*Super Strategies for*

# Succeeding on the Standardized Tests:

## Reading/Language Arts

**by Sara Davis Powell**

SCHOLASTIC
PROFESSIONAL BOOKS

New York • Toronto • London • Auckland • Sydney
Mexico City • New Delhi • Hong Kong

Cover design by Aartpack
Cover photograph by Oi Pin Chan
Interior Design by Sydney Wright

ISBN 0-439-04249-6
Copyright (C) 2000 by Sara Davis Powell
Printed in the USA

# TABLE OF CONTENTS

# INTRODUCTION

*Standardized tests are a fact of life in our schools. The stakes are high as people at all levels of accountability push for improved scores. There are numerous books written that address standardized testing along with practice materials. So what sets this book apart from others? Here's what you can expect:*

✳ This book is written for classroom teachers who are interested in arming students with test-taking strategies that go beyond drill and practice. Because I think teachers need the big picture of standardized test preparation, I've also included a healthy dose of general information about approaching the tests, and a wide variety of practical, classroom-ready materials. Sections called **Teacher Think-Alouds** give ideas on how to discuss topics and ways of thinking with your students. Modeling the thought process that leads to answers is extremely valuable.

✳ To make it easier for you to manage a test-preparation initiative, I've included instructions for making **Student Study Folders**, excellent tools that organize student work in a particular content area and focus student attention.

✳ This book provides an overview of how specific standardized tests can be approached in general, as well as in various language arts content areas. References are made throughout the book to how these tests assess knowledge and skills. You will find information on **TerraNova**, the **Metropolitan Achievement Test** (MAT), the **Comprehensive Test of Basic Skills** (CTBS), the **California Achievement Test** (CAT), the **Iowa Test of Basic Skills** (ITBS), and the **Stanford Achievement Test** (SAT), along with the specific formats they use.

✳ Throughout, you'll find **sample test items** and accompanying **teaching points** that discuss frequent errors made by students and explanations to share with students about why the answers are what they are as opposed to other options.

✳ **Student practice pages** may be used in a variety of ways—during whole-class and small-group study, or individually. They are prefaced with explanations for teachers and instructions for assisting students as they work.

✳ **Strategy suggestions** follow each major language arts topic. These pages may be photocopied as references for each student.

## The Place of Test Prep in Your Classroom

### XI. Thou Shalt Not Teach to the Test

Moses had good reasons for not including this commandment with the original ten! Because states and districts place so much confidence in test results, school status and even funding depend on the percentages generated by student performance on standardized tests. Whether or not we agree with the concept of standardized testing, this "rite of spring" takes place each year and, as teachers, we need a plan of action to prepare students for the tests.

Ideally, what we teach is what we test. Within our curriculum, we teachers can harmonize the content of our instruction and assessments. Content and assessment are not always so easy to balance when it comes to standardized testing.

The challenge is to prepare students adequately for these tests while maintaining the integrity of our own curriculum and teaching philosophy. This book will show you that it is possible to do both. First, let's take a look at some of the key points of discussion—and debate— about standardized tests, and what I think our stance ought to be.

## How much test prep should take place?

While standardized testing is a reality for all students, the levels of preparation that schools offer varies greatly. Many school districts base their prescribed level of preparation on the continuum developed by Mehrens and Kaminski, which consists of seven initiatives. Test preparation might include:

**1.** general instruction on objectives of the curriculum

**2.** instruction on test-taking skills

**3.** instruction on objectives generated by looking at the objectives measured by a variety of standardized tests

**4.** instruction on objectives generated specifically to match the skills involved in the standardized test to be used

**5.** instruction on specifically matched skills in which instruction follows the same item format as the test questions

**6.** practice on a parallel form of the test to be used

**7.** practice on the actual test to be used

States and districts tend to view test preparation as an ethical issue. Some only endorse the first two levels while others encourage levels 1-6. By not agreeing on an acceptable level of preparation we are unfairly comparing student performance. Levels 1-6 should be viewed as not only ethical, but also desirable. We teach our students to prepare, to study, to rehearse. These are life lessons. In sports, in math, in performance arts, we practice for the "real thing." Basketball players spend hours shooting hoops. During a game, moves practiced are applied under "test" conditions. Students practice not only necessary computation for story problems, but also the possible strategies needed to sequence and frame the computation within context to arrive at the solution. If a standardized test is the "real thing," shouldn't we parallel it as closely as possible in the preparation?

The fact that educators don't agree on levels of preparation isn't surprising, given that to begin with they don't agree on the value of standardized tests. Many educators criticize standardized testing, believing that it drives the curriculum and leads to excessive drill and practice. Some feel that the typical multiple choice format disallows higher order thinking. Still others see the tests as culturally biased or not accurate measures of what children know and can do. There is a growing call for authentic assessment involving alternative methods that measure problem solving and task performance under "real life" situations (Hymes, 1991).

## Learn From the Results

While we continue to fight the good fight for authentic assessment and improved standardized tests, we ought to accentuate their positive aspects. Wisely using the information they do provide will go a long way toward making them useful tools of instruction. Let's look at some of the benefits of standardized testing.

Standardized tests allow us to see an overview of what our children know. They provide an opportunity for our students to apply analytical thinking and problem-solving strategies. While test results may be partially a reflection of how "practiced" our students are, they can still give us a basis for comparing this year's group to last year's. By analyzing the results, we can ask valuable questions about instruction. Did a particular group score consistently from one year to the next? If not, did the staff change? Was more or less time spent on direct preparation? Were different textbooks used? Did the test show areas of weakness in the content we teach? Are there gaps? What skills do we need to emphasize? Rather than dismissing results, we can use them to examine and track change and progress.

## Help Kids Get Used to Being Tested

To increase student comfort level with standardized format, "practice tests" should be given often throughout the year. These may be generic, grade-level-specific tests from a publisher, or teacher-made tests covering current curriculum. The important thing is to create a standardized test environment complete with a variety of test formats as well as behavioral expectations.

The results of the practice tests should be reviewed with the students and used as indicators of strengths and weaknesses. Developing a scheme or organizational structure that allows students to chart their own progress fosters independence and encourages students to take responsibility for their own learning. As students become familiar with the process, their performance will improve. They will become confident and anxieties will lessen as the "routineness" of testing and reflecting sets in. This kind of paper and pencil testing will not detract from more innovative means of assessment, but will help maintain balance.

The following chapters show you how to model important test-taking strategies, making them explicit for students, and then provide practice pages for students to apply these strategies on their own.

# CHAPTER 1

# Teaching Test-Wise Skills

It is beneficial to equip students with test-taking skills. Life is full of tests. Being able to get to the heart of what is asked rather than floundering with format issues lets kids show what they know. Test-taking skills can be incorporated daily into our planned curriculum. It would be a disservice to only concentrate on the format style we know will be used on this year's chosen standardized tests. To increase students' flexibility, it is important to expose them to a variety of instructional and assessment modes.

The following strategies represent a variety of ways we can help students prepare for standardized tests. Address them with students in the context of the reading/language arts test prep activites described in later chapters. Some of the strategies may seem to come from opposing viewpoints while others complement each other. The goal is to expose students to an array of test-taking strategies to increase their awareness and flexibility. You may find it useful to put a tally mark next to a strategy when you emphasize it in order to see if there are gaps. Add to the list to personalize it for your students.

## Test-Taking Strategies

### Strategies for understanding the importance of tests

Help kids appreciate that tests allow us to:

_____ show what we know

_____ derive satisfaction from successful test results

_____ enhance school spirit

_____ improve community perception

### Strategies for practicing in a simulated test environment

_____ follow oral directions

_____ maintain silence during testing

## Strategies for learning to manage time

_____use timed tests in the classroom

_____check answers after completing section

_____pace according to number of items and allotted time

## Strategies for learning to deal with answer choices

_____ practice with multiple choice questions

_____ consider all answer choices

_____ take a good guess (if there's no penalty)

_____ try answer choices in context of problems

_____ eliminate answer choices (probability lesson!)

_____ recognize detractors

_____ recognize when correct answer is not given

_____ answer every question

## Strategies for using the test booklet

_____ mark choices in booklet (if allowed)

_____ mark difficult questions to remind to go back

_____ underline key words/phrases

_____ cross out extraneous information

_____ use problems as written in the booklet rather than rewriting

## Strategies for dealing with reading passages

_____ read questions before reading passage

_____ refer to passage to find answers

_____ recognize and use key words/phrases (scanning)

_____ practice with both long and short passages

# 10 Test-Taking Tips for Students

1. Quickly scan the test section. This will give you an idea of what's coming in the time allowed for the section.

2. Learn to manage your time. Look at your watch or the wall clock to figure out when half, and then all, of your time is up. After scanning the test section you will have an idea of where you should be when half the time is gone in order to finish.

3. Listen carefully as your teacher reads the directions.

4. Answer all the test questions. Most standardized tests do not take off for guessing.

5. When you come to a very difficult question, eliminate answer choices that you know are wrong.

6. When faced with a fill-in-the-blank question, try all the answer choices to see which one is best.

7. Do not spend too much time on any one item. If you skip an item and plan to go back later, make sure you leave the answer space blank.

8. If you finish early, go back and check your answers or answer items you may have left out. Remember that often your first thoughts are most likely to be correct.

9. Be sure to get enough sleep the night before the test.

10. Remember that tests give you opportunities to show what you know!

# Teacher Test-Wiseness: Tips for Success

No matter where on the preparation continuum your school policy falls, there are some proactive steps you can take to help students boost their scores and learn more content and skills along the way:

**1.** Make the idea of test preparation just another layer of motivation to do our best for children. Keep the test in mind all year long. Don't wait until February—interweave test objectives from day one.

**2.** Continually strive to present a broad and comprehensive curriculum. The publishers of standardized tests select from a wide variety of sources when writing test items.

**3.** Create enthusiasm. Our attitudes as teachers have a direct bearing on the attitudes of our students. If we approach standardized testing as an evil to be dreaded, or at best endured, our children will do the same. Have a poster contest and a pep rally. Encourage students to write poems and rap songs to help build motivation.

**4.** Reading is the key factor in all areas of standardized tests. So get your kids to read, read, read ... anything from comic strips to classic literature, from cereal boxes to technical instruction manuals. Ask for paraphrasing, opinions, predictions, analysis—all the things that call for comprehension.

**5.** Emphasize vocabulary in all subject areas. A rich vocabulary list will contain math, science, language arts, and social studies terms, as well as words found in typical spelling books or at the end of stories in literature books. Post a list every week of words your students will encounter in your planned curriculum. Use these words often, point to them with a colorful "vocab wand"—ham it up! Challenge your students to find them in the newspaper. Have them write notes to each other (they're going to do it anyway!) using as many of the words as they can.

**6.** Show students that the whole world of words is at their finger tips through insistence on frequent use of the dictionary, thesaurus, and book glossaries. These tools allow students to explore meanings and discover that many words actually have multiple meanings.

**7.** Have students edit their own work and others' writing. Every grammar lesson that needs to be taught can be encompassed in editing assignments that have much more meaning for students than isolated examples and one-sentence practice.

**8.** One of our goals is to increase student flexibility and decrease the apprehension students feel. Let's teach and test in a variety of ways to stretch our students' potential and help them feel less intimidated by tests.

**9.** Use published test-preparation materials as much as your state or district will allow. You may need to make your own materials using common sense and whatever you remember from previous experiences. Most of us have shelves jam-packed with practice materials in all kinds of formats.

# Managing Test Prep: Use Student Study Folders

Since our ultimate goal is to create independent, lifelong learners, the way we incorporate test-taking skills into the curriculum should reflect that ideal. However, busy teachers working with an already full curriculum do not need any add-ons to their packed schedules. An easy and effective way to manage test prep while fostering independent learning is to introduce student study folders. This management strategy places the responsibility for learning on the student, who maintains and updates the folders.

Have students create study folders for each content area. It is helpful if the entire class uses the same color folder for each subject, and that each subject has its own color. Two-pocket folders with inside fasteners to hold three-hole-punched papers are ideal. These folders are often reasonably priced during back-to-school sales, so add six folders per student to your beginning-of-the-year school supply list.

In the folders, students place testing strategies specific to each content-area test, completed practice tests and activities, and study guides. The folders should contain the curriculum objectives and standards that you would teach with or without standardized tests, emphasizing that the knowledge and skills learned have importance beyond just the test. In fact, stress to students that the tests provide them with an opportunity to show what they know—to demonstrate that they can apply what they've learned. In this way, the study folders become an integral part of each subject.

Once your students have created their study folders, use them consistently. We are all creatures of habit, so consciously make using the study folders a habit for the whole class. When you provide a handout you want students to keep for reference, remind them to store it in their study folders. Encourage students to use the folders as resources during their daily work. Routinely review test-taking strategies, conduct practice tests, and suggest that students store completed work in the folders. Consistently update and revise study guides and strategy tips. Most important, establish routines that you feel comfortable with and that complement your content-area instruction.

Keep in mind that the number of content sections that fit comfortably in one folder will depend on students' needs and grade level. A fourth-grade class may require an entire folder for capitalization and punctuation practice, while an eighth-grade class may need just a small part of a comprehensive language arts mechanics folder for that topic. Carefully diagnosing the previous year's test results of an incoming class will help you decide how to structure the folders. A class may show such distinct weaknesses in dictionary skills that an entire folder may need to be designated for this skill. Of course, as the year goes on the folder structure may be changed as necessary; adapt the tool to your needs.

## A Sample Folder

Here is an example of what a folder might include and how it could be organized:

☒ Content-specific curriculum objectives and standards—three-hole-punched and stored in the middle section

☒ Content-specific strategy suggestions (photocopied from this book)—three-hole-punched and stored in middle

☒ Study notes and sample tests (from this book or teacher generated)—stored in left pocket

☒ Completed practice tests (from this book and supplemented as needed)—stored in right pocket

☒ Color-coded content sections—all strategy suggestions, examples and notes, and practice tests on a subject, say, capitalization and punctuation, could be coded for quick access with green stars drawn by students

## Management Tip

Set aside time for students to design a cover pattern for their study folders. Let them have fun with it! This engenders ownership, and students are more likely to keep up with the folder because they have pride in what they have done to make it their own. Small things like this make a big difference to kids in the middle grades!

# CHAPTER 2

# Vocabulary: Building Word Power

We begin learning words the instant we are born (some propose that this process starts "in utero"!) and continue to build our word banks throughout our lives. The spoken, heard, read, and written word is an instrument of learning, a vehicle of information, and a changer of history. It can bolster or destroy, encourage or inhibit, entice or bore—the list is as long as the lexicon itself. If we accept the importance of words, then a broad and comprehensive vocabulary has power that cannot be underestimated; clearly, vocabulary study deserves a primary place in the classroom.

Since a strong vocabulary is so important, it is not surprising that all the standardized tests devote several sections to it. The following chart outlines what may be expected in the vocabulary sections of some of the most widely used standardized tests.

## Vocabulary Content on Standardized Tests

|  | TBS | | ITBS | | MAT | | SAT | | CAT | |
|---|---|---|---|---|---|---|---|---|---|---|
|  | Grades 3-5 | Grades 6-8 | Grades 3-5 | Grades 6-8 | Grades 3-5 | Grades 6-8 | Grades 3-5 | Grades 6-8 | Grades 3-5 | Grades 6-8 |
| Synonyms | X | X | X | X | X | X | X | X | X | X |
| Antonyms | X | X | X | X | X | X | 3-4 |  |  |  |
| Words in Context | X | X | X | X | X | X | X | X | X | X |
| Derivation | X | X |  | X |  | X | X | X |  |  |
| Affix Meanings |  | X |  | X | X | X | X | X | X |  |
| Multiple Meanings | X |  | X | X | X | X | X | X | X | X |

This chapter will provide specific strategies for approaching the vocabulary segment of standardized tests. In addition to enriching students' vocabulary base, we need to model specific strategies, including reading the directions carefully, using context clues, accessing personal experiences, and using word knowledge. The following section offers ideas for creating a word-rich classroom, and the rest of the chapter provides teacher think-alouds, group activities, and independent student practice sheets that develop vocabulary test-taking skills.

# Setting Up a Word-Rich Environment

The best way to build vocabulary is to immerse students in a word-rich environment. We can turn classrooms into such places by incorporating the ideas below. Best of all, while building the strong vocabulary students need for a rich, productive life, we are preparing them for an important section on every standardized language arts test.

As teachers we may:

- Master, use, and continually add to our own personal vocabulary. We should model this process, through think-alouds tied to personal and school texts, and by informally sharing with kids when we come across a word that intrigues us, tickles us, or intimidates us.

- Encourage students to read challenging material that will continually expose them to new words. We want them to question meanings. They should not let a single word slip by that is unclear in meaning.

- Emphasize that every discipline has its own set of words that are, in large part, specific to the discipline, while perhaps taking on a broader context when used outside the discipline. For instance, to middle-level students the word *symmetry* is probably most often associated with math. Yet we speak of art forms as having symmetry and architectural designs as possessing symmetry. From geometry lesson to drawing board, *symmetry* has contextual richness.

- Expect students to use appropriate vocabulary. They should not be allowed to routinely use easy phrases such as "top number" for *numerator* or "up and down line" for *longitude*.

- Remember that since students read fiction in language arts class and then technical explanations in science, content-specific and general-usage words both require attention.

- Establish a word power center, full of fun, vocabulary-building activities and games. Consider using flash cards. Teachers can start a classroom file of words on index cards sorted alphabetically in a pocket chart or a shoe holder hanging from a door. Students and teachers may add new and/or interesting words to the file by writing words on one side and definitions on the other side of index cards. The words can be used periodically for drills and games.

- Develop a word wall. This is a method of making words visible by posting them on the classroom wall under beginning letters. Teachers can encourage students to use the words when they speak and write.

- Obtain a list of most often used, and either misspelled or misused, words for a specific grade level. The students should be given the list. (They can place it in their vocabulary study folders for easy reference.) They may discuss the words and, in groups, write their most common mistakes and how to avoid them.

- Suggest that students compile their own personal dictionary of words that give them trouble, and new words they encounter.

- Make words come alive by providing a visual context. The adage, "A picture is worth a thousand words," may be true, but the reversal is true also: A word can stimulate a thousand pictures! Encourage students to draw pictures to accompany definitions and share pictures with the whole class.

- Generate lists of words that may apply to what the students will see, hear, and experience during an upcoming special occasion like a field trip, a concert, or a sporting event. Discussing these words ahead of time will help the occasion be more meaningful while giving a vehicle to communicate about experiences.

## Vocabulary Books to Try

### For Teachers

*Easy Mini-Lessons for Building Vocabulary* by Laura Robb (Scholastic Professional Books, 1999)

*Fab Vocab!* By Marguerite Hartill (Scholastic Professional Books, 1999)

### For Students

*A Chartreuse Leotard in a Magenta Limousine: And Other Words Named After People and Place* by Lynda Graham-Barber, illustrated by Barbara Lehman (Hyperion, 1994)

*Scholastic Dictionary of Idioms* by Marvin Terban (Scholastic, 1996)

**How do you emphasize vocabulary in your classroom?**

❋ Think About It    ❋ Ask Other Teachers    ❋ Share Ideas!

# Vocabulary Activity 1: Say It with Color

This activity fosters vocabulary development, exploration of synonyms, and identification of colorful language. It heightens awareness of word choice and provides editing practice. Specifically, it develops student awareness of colorful language, which is tested on the MAT 7, CTBS, and ITBS.

Here's how to introduce it:

1. Share the original and revised paragraphs below with students. Talk about the differences between them. Why is the second one more fun to read than the first? Make a list of the ideas generated, noting attributes such as precise language, vivid verbs, and specific things noticed by students.

## Original (Bland!) Paragraph

> I have a dog that sleeps in our yard when I'm not home. He is very nice and likes to play with me very much when I get home from school. He jumps on me and barks. He is very fast when he runs after the Frisbee I throw him.

> My adorable beagle Snoopy sleeps the days away in the shade of the giant oak tree in our front yard. But as soon as he sees me turn the corner on my way home from school, he jumps right up and bounds across the grass to greet me with wet, sloppy kisses. He pounces on me and yelps with happiness, knowing that soon we will be romping together in the back yard. Snoopy loves it when I throw my oversized orange Frisbee for him to catch. When he runs toward me with it in his mouth, it looks like he's got a big dinner plate he wants me to fill with food. Oh, and you should see how he acts at dinner time!

2. Have each student write a deliberately dull paragraph on a topic you select. Their word choices should be boring; encourage students to use dull, lackluster adjectives and adverbs or to leave modifiers out entirely. The descriptors used should be repetitive or vague.

3. Have students exchange paragraphs with neighbors for peer editing and to check only for mechanical correctness. Ask peer editors to correct errors or mark them for the writer to fix. When the paragraphs have been corrected, collect them to distribute in Step 4.

4. Put students in groups of three; heterogeneous groups work best. Give each group a paragraph to "spice up" by using colorful adjectives and adverbs, eliminating repetitive words and phrases, renaming nouns, and replacing unexciting words. (Each group should complete three paragraphs.) Groups rewrite their paragraphs and attach the new versions to the originals.

5. Have groups read aloud to the whole class both the original and the revised version of their first paragraph, encouraging discussion of the changes and choices the group made. Address the rest of the paragraphs the same way.

6. Students can mount the original and revised paragraphs on 11-by-17-inch colored paper and share them with younger children or their peers in other classes.

## Sample Sentences to Get You Started

You may find that it's actually difficult to write a boring sentence or paragraph. Here are some to use. Caution: These paragraphs may cause drowsiness. Do not read while operating the copy machine!

I got up early. I dressed and ate breakfast very fast. I ran to my friend's house very fast. I woke him up. It was the first day of summer vacation. We were going fishing.

When I get bored I get lazy. I do nothing and complain. I don't want to move even though I know that when I do, I'll find something to do and feel better.

My Aunt Betty has four cats, two dogs, chickens in the backyard, and bird feeders in all of the trees in her yard. Going to her house is fun. It is also very noisy.

## Vocabulary Activity 2: Homophone Roundup

Homophones are tricky for students of all ages, but for success in reading and writing—and on standardized tests—kids must be familiar with them. This activity asks students to generate lists of homophones and challenges them to recall unusual homophone pairs, since the team with the most pairs not on any other group's list wins. The element of competition engages all students and gets them thinking about language.

- Challenge individual students to write as many sets of homophones as they can in five minutes.

- Form groups and have members pool their words and brainstorm more words together on a master list. Call time after 15 minutes, and do not allow anyone to add words after time has been called.

- Have groups choose one person to read homophone pairs and one person to maintain the homophone list, crossing out pairs read by other groups.

- Record all student sets on chart paper. You will be writing furiously for a while! Remind students that if any other group has the same pair that is read aloud, the pair is eliminated from all group lists. The group with the most sets left at the end wins.

Here's a list of frequently used homophones:

| | | |
|---|---|---|
| sea, see | pain, pane | hole, whole |
| plane, plain | no, know | toe, tow |
| to, two, too | pale, pail | weight, wait |
| red, read | meet, meat | son, sun |
| rain, reign | heel, heal | pore, pour |

| | | |
|---|---|---|
| deer, dear | for, four | prey, pray |
| bear, bare | so, sew | knew, new |
| flour, flower | be, bee | hi, high |
| I, eye | ale, ail | sale, sail |
| wear, where | tail, tale | do, dew |
| there, their, they're | cent, sent, scent | sell, cell |
| blue, blew | right, write | or, ore |
| dye, die | hair, hare | beet, beat |

# Vocabulary Activity 3: Revise and Conquer

Using context clues to understand a word's meaning is a valuable skill for readers, and one that can be used to advantage on standardized tests. The following activity allows students to practice this skill while building their vocabulary. In this example, students find their own words in the dictionary, but you could also use your weekly vocabulary list, or have students compile words from their reading. The more you do this activity, the more comfortable students will be in "guessing" meaning based on context clues.

## *Day One*

1. Have groups of three choose three words in the dictionary that none of them have ever seen. Watch them have fun with this! They may become big Noah Webster fans when they begin to discover interesting words! What middle-school student wouldn't enjoy just pronouncing words like *onomatopoeia, gawking, burking*? Can't you just hear the giggles?

2. Have students read and discuss the definitions given for each word until each group member understands the meanings and possible contexts of the words. Be available to answer any questions that may arise.

3. Have the groups write three sentences using each word in context. The first sentence should provide limited context clues, with each subsequent sentence providing more details. The third sentence should give readers enough clues for them to determine the meaning of the word.

4. Collect and check the sentences, suggesting ways to alter them to make the meanings more obvious within context.

## Day Two

1. Allow groups time to write (or rewrite) their three sentences on transparency film.

| | |
|---|---|
| Word | .................................................................................................................................................... |
| Sentence 1 | ............................................................................................................................ |
| Sentence 2 | ............................................................................................................................ |
| Sentence 3 | ............................................................................................................................ |

2. Collect the transparencies.

3. Reveal one sentence at a time on the overhead as the whole class attempts to define the word using only context clues. Show the first sentence and allow time for students to write a definition on the form provided (see example, below). Then reveal the second sentence and encourage students to revise their definitions based on the new clues; repeat for the third sentence. Students enter their revisions on the appropriate lines; do not allow them to erase, add on to, or change any of their attempts, since the goal is to see how they use context clues.

4. Each student will complete a form for each word presented. They will make a guess at the definition when the first sentence is revealed. They will try to revise (*rewrite to make revisions*) the definition as the other context clue sentences are revealed. Students are not allowed to erase, add to, or change their three definition attempts.

| | |
|---|---|
| Word | .................................................................................................................................... |
| guessed definition | .................................................................................................................... |
| revised definition | .................................................................................................................... |
| revised definition | .................................................................................................................... |
| dictionary definition | ................................................................................................................ |
| Sentences using dictionary definition: | ................................................................................ |
| 1. | ............................................................................................................................................. |
| 2. | ............................................................................................................................................. |

5. Because the students worked in groups to originate three words with three sentences each, they will know three of the bank of items. This provides encouragement.

**6.** After the three definition attempts have been made for each word in the day's lesson, allow time for students to look up the word in the dictionary and write the first definition given.

**7.** Have students write two sentences using the word in context.

**8.** This process may be repeated during the same class period or one word may be tackled each day.

Here's an example of what the completed activity sheet might look like.

Word ..prerogative....................................................................................................................

Sentence 1 _We all have the prerogative to do something._.................................................

Sentence 2 _He had a prerogative to choose the bike._.................................................

Sentence 3 _No one could tell him not to choose the bike because it was his prerogative._
_to make the choice._....................................................................................

Word ..prerogative....................................................................................................................

guessed definition _to want to do something._.........................................................................

revised definition _to make a choice_.........................................................................................

revised definition _to decide something no matter what_........................................................

dictionary definition _the unquestionable right belonging to a person_..............................

Sentences using dictionary definition:

1. _I have the prerogative to eat or not to eat ice cream._.....................................................

2. _We shouldn't try to take someone's prerogative away._..................................................

# Synonyms and Antonyms

Some of the words students will be asked to know or figure out in vocabulary items on standardized tests will be words they hear or see often, but have never been required to actually know. Other words may be totally new to them. Some may have prefixes or suffixes or stems they have used before. In some phrases and sentences there will probably be context clues, while there may be no clues in others. To make it even more complicated, sometimes students will be asked to find a word that has the same meaning, and then other times they will be asked to find words that have the opposite meaning. Getting kids "up to speed" with synonyms and antonyms will go a long way toward improving their test performance.

To help students navigate these deceptively simple questions, we need to model the process of choosing an answer, showing students how to

☒ read directions carefully,          ☒ use context clues,

☒ draw on personal knowledge, and   ☒ use word knowledge.

We need to emphasize the importance of reading directions! Students need to realize that an antonym may fit into a sentence, but if the directions ask for a synonym then that's what they need to choose. As we do sample problems together, we need to think aloud through the process of looking for things we already know about the word and possible clues. After conducting the introductory lesson with kids, photocopy and hand out pages 24–25, Synonyms and Antonyms Teacher-Directed Student Practice. Give students time to complete the reproducible page, and then divide the class in groups of four to spend five to ten minutes talking about their strategies for arriving at each answer. Then, as a class, have groups share ideas while you write the strategies on chart paper.

## Introductory Lesson

Put the following four examples on transparencies and talk through your process of choosing an answer; a sample teacher think-aloud is provided for each question.

**1. Directions:** Choose the word or phrase that means the same, or nearly the same, as the underlined word.

| | |
|---|---|
| **Example:** | mountain <u>peak</u> |
| | A. valley     C. top |
| | B. slope      D. side |

### ◎ Think-Aloud

Say to students, "The first thing I want to do is see if any of the choices just plain sound wrong. Mountain *valley* ... I think this is probably not right because a mountain is tall and a valley is low.

So I think *valley* is not a very good choice. Maybe mountain *slope*? In the winter I watch a lot of sports on TV and I know people ski on slopes. Mountain *top*—mountains have tops, don't they? And sides, too! Hmmm...I remember my friend talks about going to the woods to see the leaves in autumn. She calls it 'the peak of the season.' I guess she means *the best*. If something is *best*, it's at the top.... So I think *peak* means *top*."

**2. Directions:** Choose the word or phrase that means the same, or nearly the same, as the word in bold type.

Example:     **discontinue** the newspaper
A. buy          C. burn
B. read         D. cancel

## Think-Aloud

"Well, I think all four of these things can be done to a newspaper, so I can't eliminate any of the choices. But...I see *dis* a lot. It usually means to *undo* something. To *continue* something means to *keep it up.* Teachers say it a lot! So if I combine *dis* and *continue*... I heard the principal say we had to cancel our field trip, so we didn't go. It makes sense that *discontinue* means *cancel*."

**3. Directions:** Choose the word or phrase that means the opposite of the word in bold type.

Example:     I'm going to the **final** game tonight.
A. last          C. exciting
B. first         D. next to the last

## Think-Aloud

"I see the word *opposite* in the directions. I know how important it is to read the directions! I'm glad I did this time! I know that *final* means *last* and I would have chosen A if I had not read the directions. The opposite of *last* is *first*, so *first* must also be the opposite of *final*. Let me think that through one more time... Yes, B is correct."

**4. Directions:** Choose the word that means the same, or nearly the same, as the underlined word in the sentence.

Example:     We were surprised that the large dog was <u>docile</u>.
A. aggressive     C. smelly
B. gentle         D. peppy

## Think-Aloud

"Let's see. A large dog could be any of these things. Would I be surprised if a large dog was aggressive? I think I can use *surprised* as a context clue. It will help me figure out what *docile* means. I'm not sure what *aggressive* means, so I'll come back to that. How about *gentle*? The large dogs I have been around don't make me think of gentle, but I remember that they were smelly and jumped on me, which means they were peppy, so I'll rule out *peppy* and *smelly*. Since I would be surprised that a big dog would be gentle, I think that *docile* means the same as *gentle*. Even though I'm still not sure what *aggressive* means, I think I've arrived at the correct answer, with the help of the context clue."

**Teacher-Directed Student Practice**

# Synonyms and Antonyms

This practice asks you to think about why you chose a particular synonym or antonym. Check the box or boxes beside the statement(s) that best describes what helped you make up your mind. Your teacher will lead a class discussion of the items.

**Directions:** Choose the word or phrase that means the same, or nearly the same, as the underlined word.

**1.** <u>vandalized</u> apartment
a  neat and orderly
b  wrecked
c  spacious
d  hidden

I decided on my answer because:
_____ I know the word.
_____ I know a word like it.
_____ I can eliminate some choices.
_____ I've heard the word used.
_____ I guessed!
_____ other

**2.** <u>subtle</u> sense of humor
a  spontaneous
b  malicious
c  refined
d  grim

I decided on my answer because:
_____ I know the word.
_____ I know a word like it.
_____ I can eliminate some choices.
_____ I've heard the word used.
_____ I guessed!
_____ other

**3.** <u>adorn</u> the Christmas tree
a  take down or remove
b  decorate or embellish
c  gaze upon
d  appreciate

I decided on my answer because:
_____ I know the word.
_____ I know a word like it.
_____ I can eliminate some choices.
_____ I've heard the word used.
_____ I guessed!
_____ other

**4.** <u>exploit</u> the occasion
a  take advantage of
b  retreat from
c  leave alone
d  enjoy

I decided on my answer because:
_____ I know the word.
_____ I know a word like it.
_____ I can eliminate some choices.
_____ I've heard the word used.
_____ I guessed!
_____ other

**Teacher-Directed Student Practice**

# Synonyms and Antonyms (Cont.)

Student
Page

**Directions:** Choose the word or phrase that means the opposite of the word in bold type.

**5. infinite** opportunities
a  rare and precious
b  dull and ordinary
c  boundless
d  limited

I decided on my answer because:
_____ I know the word.
_____ I know a word like it.
_____ I can eliminate some choices.
_____ I've heard the word used.
_____ I guessed!
_____ other

**6. nonchalant** attitude
a  cool and casual
b  careless
c  enthusiastic
d  spiteful

I decided on my answer because:
_____ I know the word.
_____ I know a word like it.
_____ I can eliminate some choices.
_____ I've heard the word used.
_____ I guessed!
_____ other

**7. socially prominent**
a  attention-grabber
b  proud
c  inconspicuous
d  shy and timid

I decided on my answer because:
_____ I know the word.
_____ I know a word like it.
_____ I can eliminate some choices.
_____ I've heard the word used.
_____ I guessed!
_____ other

**8. enticing** dessert
a  intriguing
b  moist and delicious
c  overly sweet
d  repellent

I decided on my answer because:
_____ I know the word.
_____ I know a word like it.
_____ I can eliminate some choices.
_____ I've heard the word used.
_____ I guessed!
_____ other

**Independent Practice: Phrases**

# Synonyms and Antonyms

Student
Page

**Directions:** Choose the word or phrase that means the same, or nearly the same, as the underlined word.

**1.** <u>courageous</u> knight
   A. full of hope      C. brave
   B. muscular          D. cowardly

**2.** <u>dismal</u> weather
   A. hot               C. cloudy
   B. gloomy            D. cold

**3.** <u>scholarly</u> teacher
   A. mean              C. refined
   B. tall and beautiful  D. smart

**4.** <u>humorous</u> story
   A. laughable         C. boring
   B. short and sweet   D. foolish

**Directions:** Think carefully about the meaning of the word in the bold type. Then choose a word that means the opposite.

**5. superb** movie
   A. dreadful          C. funny
   B. sad               D. excellent

**6. muffled** by the blanket
   A. softened          C. quieted
   B. comforted         D. made louder

**7. beneficial** activity
   A. tiring            C. harmful
   B. fun               D. relaxing

**8. absurd** tale
   A. ridiculous        C. witty
   B. believable        D. sad

Name _____ Date _____

Independent Practice: Sentences

# Synonyms and Antonyms

**Directions:** Choose the word that means the same, or nearly the same, meaning as the underlined word in each sentence.

**1.** The teacher asked the students to <u>extend</u> the line.
 A. shorten        C. lengthen
 B. erase          D. cat

**2.** We were afraid he would make a <u>grave</u> mistake as he worked very quickly.
 E. foolish        G. honest
 F. sudden         H. serious

**3.** Although we tried very hard, we were told that it was a <u>futile</u> attempt.
 A. hopeless       C. dangerous
 B. brave          D. final

**4.** Before we started to play, the coach said we had to <u>discuss</u> the rules.
 E. learn          G. dislike
 F. write down     H. talk over

**5.** It was hard to believe her <u>incredible</u> story.
 A. imaginary      C. dislike
 B. unbelievable   D. true

**6.** Even though it was getting dark, we were told to continue to watch <u>intently</u>.
 E. angrily        G. attentively
 F. silently       H. secretly

**7.** We tried to <u>convince</u> a friend to help us at the carnival.
 A. promise        C. visit
 B. ask            D. persuade

**8.** Not only was the shipment of high quality, it also boasted <u>infinite</u> variety.
 E. imitation      G. unlimited
 F. colorful       H. detailed

• Vocabulary words and synonym choices from *How to be a Better Test Taker* published by Scholastic, Inc. 1984.

# Multiple Meaning Words

Many standardized tests assess knowledge of words with multiple meanings in the vocabulary section. We know that multiple meaning words pose unique problems to students, and we try to call attention to them when we come across them in discussions, on assignments, and in our reading. The words themselves are rarely difficult—kids even enjoy exploring different meanings—but on standardized tests students often seem to lose what they know about multiple meaning words because of the unfamiliar format of the questions.

To prepare kids, concentrate awhile on the language of the directions and format, and model the strategies that allow students to show their knowledge of multiple meaning words. The following section presents some sample teacher think-alouds that help students to confidently address multiple meaning word questions.

## Introductory Lesson

You might say to students, "We know that some words have more than one meaning. Let's name some of them."

Write words on chalkboard or chart paper as students suggest them. After each word, ask for volunteers to give different meanings. After discussing several words, tell students they will probably encounter multiple meaning words on their standardized test in the spring, and that you are going to practice some test questions so they won't get tripped up by unusual directions.

[Put the following example on a transparency so you can show what to do with your pencil— crossing out choices.]

---

**Directions:** Choose the word whose meanings fit both sentences.

I asked him not to _____ the glass.

It looks like there is only one _____ left.

    A. drink      C. drop

    B. cup       D. break

---

### ⊚ Think-Aloud

"Okay, it says to choose the word whose meanings fit both sentences. There's that word—*both*—which alerts me to make sure my choice works in both sentences. I know that two or three of the possible answers will work fine in *one* of the sentences, but only one word will fit *both* sentences. I'm going to cover the second sentence with the pencil.

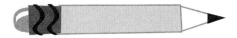

I asked him not to _____ the glass.

Now I'm going to try each choice in the first sentence:

*I asked him not to drink the glass.* Well, I know I can drink what's in the glass, but not actually drink the glass. So A is wrong. I'll lightly cross through the A. No matter how well it might fit the second sentence, A cannot be the answer.

❧ *I asked him not to cup the glass.* This doesn't sound right. So B is wrong. I'll cross through it with my pencil.

❧ *I asked him not to drop the glass.* That fits! So choice C is a possibility.

❧ Well, choice D—*I asked him not to break the glass*—fits, too. So I have two possibilities. Choices C and D are the ones I'll test in the second sentence.

❧ Now I'll cover the first sentence with my pencil so I can focus better on the second sentence:

It looks like there is only one _____ left.

❧ *It looks like there is only one drop left.* That's fine! But I'm going to check D before I mark my answer.

❧ *It looks like there is only one break left.* No, that isn't right. I'm going to choose C!"

After conducting a think-aloud that demonstrates how to approach these questions, write another sample problem (see pages 32–33) on the board and invite a student to think aloud his or her process of finding the correct answer. Then, as a class, work through the teacher-directed student practice on the following page.

**Teacher-Directed Student Practice**

# Multiple Meaning Words

**Directions:** Choose the word whose meanings fit both sentences.

1. Please do this_____for her.
Do you_____the red balloon?
A. task          C. like
B. want          D. favor

2. We saw the_____do tricks.
Before you mail the envelope, remember to_____it.
E. close         G. fill
F. seal          H. dog

3. The oil was_____into gasoline.
She was very proper and _____.
A. wealthy       C. turned
B. converted     D. refined

4. The western shirt had a_____missing.
You should_____those twigs to make them fit.
E. snap          G. break
F. button        H. pocket

## Discussion Pointers

- Point out to students that using a pencil to cover a sentence will help them focus and avoid mistakes.
- Pause after reading the problem or asking a question.
- Demonstrate crossing out eliminated choices.
- Remind students to watch for key words in the directions.
- Ask questions about what makes sense, or "sounds right."
- Reinforce vocabulary by probing for meanings of words not chosen.

## Prompts to Guide Students

Use the following kinds of questions as you discuss each test example with kids. Remember to give students time to think about each of your questions, so those who aren't as quick to process information won't feel rushed. Here is how I would lead a discussion about item 1:

★ Put your pencil over the second sentence in item 1. Now read the first sentence with all four word choices.

★ Who can tell me the words that make sense in this sentence? [*task* and *favor*]

★ Lightly put a line through B and C, since we're eliminating these from consideration.

★ Now cover the first sentence with your pencil and read the second sentence, trying A and D only. Does it make sense to say, *Do you task the red balloons?* [No; the answer is *favor*.]

★ By the way, does anyone know what *task* means? Yes, it means a *job* or a *chore*. The answer is *favor*. Can you think of another meaning for *favor*? [*party favor*.]

★ Can any one tell me what *want* means? How about the word *like*? Now we're ready to move on to our next examples.

**Teacher-Directed Student Practice**

# Multiple Meaning Words

Student
Page

**Directions:** Choose the word whose meanings fit both sentences.

**1.** Please do this _____ for her.

Do you _____ the red balloon?
- A. task
- B. want
- C. like
- D. favor

**2.** We saw the _____ do tricks.

Before you mail the envelope, remember to _____ it.
- E. close
- F. seal
- G. fill
- H. dog

**3.** The oil was _____ into gasoline.

She was very proper and _____ .
- A. wealthy
- B. converted
- C. turned
- D. refined

**4.** The western shirt had a _____ missing.

You should _____ those twigs to make them fit.
- E. snap
- F. button
- G. break
- H. pocket

Independent Practice 1

# Multiple Meaning Words

Student Page

**Directions:** Choose the word whose meanings fit both sentences.

**1.** I wish you wouldn't _____ your voice.
How much money did we _____ for our new club?
- A. lower
- B. raise
- C. spend
- D. collect

**2.** We can use this _____ to measure that table.
A new _____ was elected by the people to govern their country.
- E. yardstick
- F. king
- G. ruler
- H. president

**3.** He hurt his _____ when he ran into the door.
Try to put this thread through the _____ of that needle.
- A. knee
- B. opening
- C. eye
- D. tip

**4.** A statement should be followed by a _____.
The class _____ seemed to pass slowly.
- E. question mark
- F. decade
- G. period
- H. time

**5.** What a difficult _____ she had with today's math test.
At what _____ will you be home?
- A. point
- B. time
- C. period
- D. decision

**6.** Gasoline, oil, and diesel fuel are all _____ from petroleum.
Mrs. Dupont came from an old and _____ family.
- E. wealthy
- F. made
- G. refined
- H. established

**7.** We had to _____ the dense undergrowth to reach the old camp.
The old blacksmith still fashioned horseshoes on his _____.
- A. force
- B. go
- C. stove
- D. forge

**8.** You should always _____ an agreement with a handshake.
Be sure you _____ the plastic storage bag, so it won't leak.
- E. seal
- F. clamp
- G. use
- H. fill

## Independent Practice 2

# Multiple Meaning Words

**Student Page**

**Directions:** Choose the word whose meanings fit both sentences.

1. The children always _____ from the car when we stop for snacks.
   The _____ of lightning came so close to us.
   - A. race
   - B. bolt
   - C. flash
   - D. hurry

2. My mother uses a special fingernail _____ when she does her nails.
   Our teacher always has us stand in single _____ before going to the bus.
   - E. file
   - F. rows
   - G. gloss
   - H. cream

3. How many records did the singer _____ last year?
   I love to go to the _____ aisle to see what is fresh.
   - A. design
   - B. fish
   - C. perform
   - D. produce

4. Susan got a new fishing _____ for her birthday.
   The sudden turn made me _____ and fall off the seat of the bus.
   - E. rod
   - F. jump
   - G. reel
   - H. shout

5. We waited for the bell to _____ before going home.
   She found her _____ right where you said.
   - A. pen
   - B. sound
   - C. sweater
   - D. ring

6. What will you _____ on our vacation?
   The old trunk showed signs of _____ .
   - E. want
   - F. take
   - G. wear
   - H. abuse

7. She turned the _____ on.
   It was easy to carry because it was _____ .
   - A. TV
   - B. light
   - C. small
   - D. lamp

8. This floor appears to be _____ .
   Did anyone else hear that loud _____ ?
   - E. noise
   - F. flat
   - G. sound
   - H . level

# Words in Paragraphs

Vocabulary exercises that ask students to fill in blanks in a paragraph are common on standardized tests and present special problems for many students. First of all, the paragraph looks overwhelming. Poor readers are not so daunted by phrases and single sentences, but faced with a whole paragraph, some are reminded of reading comprehension exercises that they view as discouraging! Add the numbered blanks and they may panic. Practice and familiarity become vital if students are to succeed. They must be guided through the use of context clues.

## Introductory Lesson

Put the following paragraph on a transparency.

> Emma Barrett began playing the piano at age seven and became one of this country's more important jazz ___(1)___. When she was sixty-nine, she suffered a stroke that ___(2)___ her left side. One year later, she was playing again. This time, however, she was sitting in a ___(3)___. Even so, she played with tremendous power. Emma died on January 28, 1983, ten days after her extraordinary ___(4)___ at Preservation Hall.

Say to students, "Today we are going to work on using context clues to fill in missing words in a paragraph. Each paragraph has several blanks for you to fill in, and for each blank you will have four choices. This sounds harder than it is! Listen in as I 'think aloud' through a sample. Listen carefully and follow my train of thought."

### ◉ Think-Aloud

"First, I'm going to read the whole paragraph before I even look at the word choices." (Read it aloud.)

"Now I know what the paragraph is about—an old lady who played the piano. She got sick, kept playing, and then died ... I'm ready to think about what words go in the blanks! I'm going to read the first sentence again and think about the word choices.

> Emma Barrett began playing the piano at age seven and became one of this country's more important jazz ___(1)___.
> My choices for (1) are:  A. writers    C. musicians
>                          B. ladies     D. readers

Let's see...If I put *writers* and *readers* in the blank it doesn't make much sense, so I'll cross those out. Jazz writers and jazz readers don't make much sense. I suppose you could say *jazz ladies*, but the best word is *jazz musicians*, because *jazz* refers to music. Now let's look at the second sentence.

> When she was sixty-nine, she suffered a stroke that ___(2)___ her left side.

I remember when my grandma had a stroke. I didn't understand exactly what it was, but I knew she had a hard time getting around. I'm going to look at the choices now.

My choices for (2) are:   A. lifted     C. turned
                          B. played     D. paralyzed

The word *suffered* in the sentence tells me that a stroke is bad. *Lifted* and *played* don't seem bad and they also don't make much sense, so I'll cross them out. I need to read the sentence again with *turned* and *paralyzed*.

**When she was sixty-nine, she suffered a stroke that turned her left side.**

I guess it would be bad if her left side was turned, and her right side wasn't. But it still doesn't make much sense. The word *paralyzed* is a big word. I remember seeing it in one of our R.L. Stine books. It had something to do with being afraid. I'm not sure that fits here, but I know in the story it was a bad thing. So I'm going to choose *paralyzed*, choice D."

After modeling two problems, have students work together in pairs to complete the sample paragraph. When students finish, encourage them to share the process they followed to get to their answer.

This time, however, she was sitting in a ___(3)___.
   A. bed
   B. wheelchair
   C. wagon
   D. bathtub

Emma died on January 28, 1983, ten days after her extraordinary ___(4)___ at Preservation Hall.
   A. performance
   B. speech
   C. party
   D. doctor's appointment

From p. 27 *How to Be a Better Test Taker*, Scholastic, Inc. 1984.

# Words in Paragraphs: Pair Practice Activity

Have students work with a partner to decide on the correct word for each blank in the paragraph. Ensure students follow these steps:

**1.** One partner reads the first paragraph while the other listens. Then they change roles for the second paragraph.
**2.** Talk together about what the paragraphs are about.
**3.** Go through the blanks, one at a time. Cross out incorrect answers, and use context clues and word knowledge to choose your answer.
**4.** Make a decision on each blank together, and be able to discuss why you chose your answer.

**Directions:** Choose the words that best fit the numbered blanks in the following paragraphs.

Water covers three-fourths of the Earth's surface. This large body of water can be divided into four oceans—Pacific, Atlantic, Indian, and Artic—of which the Pacific is the largest and deepest and the Artic is the smallest and shallowest. Ocean water contains many dissolved ____(1)____ including salt, gold, and silver. The minerals are washed into streams and rivers and carried out into the ocean.

  The ocean is in a constant ____(2)____ of movement. Waves, caused by wind blowing across the surface, can ____(3)____ in height from less than one inch (ripples) to over 100 feet, depending on how hard and long the wind blows. Ocean currents are warm or cold ____(4)____ movements of water also caused by wind. Tides are the regular rising and falling of ocean waters caused by the shifting pull of ____(5)____ as the moon revolves around the Earth.

  The ocean has ____(6)____ of plant and animal life which supports a large and active fishing industry.

| | | |
|---|---|---|
| 1. A. elements | 3. A. drop | 5. A. magnetism |
| B. minerals | B. happen | B. winds |
| C. vegetables | C. stand | C. temperature |
| D. compounds | D. range | D. gravity |
| | | |
| 2. A. state | 4. A. rapid | 6. A. an abundance |
| B. city | B. horizontal | B. a source |
| C. type | C. smelly | C. a mountain |
| D. area | D. vertical | D. a surface |

From *The Complete Geography Project Activity Books*, Scholastic, Inc. 1993.

**Independent Practice**

# Words in Paragraphs

**Student
Page**

**Directions:** Choose the word that best fits each numbered blank in the following paragraph.

A screaming, whistling wind whipped in from the sea. Sheets of salt spray poured over the Orkney Islands. For two days and nights, the storm ___(1)___ these tiny islands that lie off Scotland's northeast coast!

At last, on the third day, the winds dropped and the icy rain turned to a light drizzle. The people of Mainland Island came out from their stone houses to ___(2)___ the damage.

Driftwood, seaweed, and the shattered hulls of fishing boats ___(3)___ the shore. This was a usual sight after a storm. But what the people had not expected to see were the remains of a ___(4)___ village!

The powerful surf had washed away tons of sand to uncover a group of low stone houses, all connected by stone walls and alleys. Inside the roofless buildings were stone beds, stone benches, and little stone closets with stone knives and axes.

The houses apparently had been abandoned in ___(5)___, for a necklace was found near a doorway, as if dropped there by accident.

When did it happen? Historians think this village was ___(6)___ and covered by sand some 5,000 years ago! But why? No one knows for sure.

**1.** A concealed
   B startled
   C reduced
   D lashed

**2.** A experience
   B survey
   C conceive
   D produce

**3.** A littered
   B drowned
   C clouded
   D layered

**4.** A modern
   B huge
   C prehistoric
   D complete

**5.** A darkness
   B haste
   C confusion
   D short

**6.** A found
   B built
   C populated
   D deserted

• From p. 21 *How to Be a Better Test Taker*, Scholastic, Inc. 1984.

# Strategy Suggestions

**Synonym:** a word that has the same or nearly the same meaning

**Antonym:** a word of opposite meaning

**1** Always read directions carefully. Some tests ask for synonyms and some ask for antonyms.

**2** If asked to find a synonym or antonym for a word that is in a phrase or a sentence, consider the context. Sometimes there will be no context clues, but if there are some, be sure to use them.

**3** Eliminate the obviously wrong choices by crossing them out with your pencil. Then choose from words that remain.

**4** For multiple-meaning items, make sure the word you choose fits both sentences. Begin by eliminating the words that do not fit the first sentence. Try only the remaining words in the second sentence.

**5** When you come across a new word in your schoolwork or leisure reading, stop and look it up in the dictionary. Think of ways to use the word and then make it your own.

Other strategies I use: _____

_____

_____

_____

_____

_____

_____

_____

# CHAPTER 3

# Reading Comprehension

The adage that children "learn to read" in kindergarten through third grade, and then "read to learn" from grades four on, is a generalization that all of us would love to be accurate. The truth is, students in grades four or six or even eight may still be learning to read. Many students in those grades can be considered emergent readers. We are also painfully aware that a substantial segment of our population is functionally illiterate. Making assumptions about reading proficiency based on the grade level of a student is a mistake. Today, almost all teachers are faced with the dilemma of providing reading instruction to a heterogeneous classroom of students—some of whom struggle to read words, much less comprehend meaning, others of whom are proficient and move in and out of a variety of literature with ease.

It is important for students to understand that there are actually three purposes for reading: reading for enjoyment, reading for information, and reading to perform a task. In elementary school, the majority of reading assignments and opportunities involve literacy experiences and encourage a love of reading. Many students are thrown off balance when they sense a shift from reading stories to reading for information needed to learn specific content and reading to enable them to perform a task.

Because reading with comprehension is the foundation of all content areas, it is vital that the diversity of needs relating to this most basic of skills be met. Ashley and Suzanne Bishop commented that, "To be successful readers, students must develop their own understanding of how our language works and be able to decode so fluently and naturally that all their attention is on comprehension." Those who decode fluently will need minimal instruction and will have many opportunities to practice their comprehension skills. For those who struggle with decoding, our goal should be to motivate them and provide skill instruction within a context that will be meaningful—one that will give students reasons to want to read. Isolated skill instruction will not motivate, and may actually lead to student disengagement from the reading process. It is always advisable for teachers to have as many "tools in their instructional tool boxes" as possible. What follows are suggestions for engaging middle level students in their journey toward becoming readers who "read to learn."

# Suggestions for Creating a Literature-Rich Classroom

Students will be motivated by the attractiveness of books and other reading materials if they are displayed in interesting ways. Pictures of authors, student reviews, illustrations, dioramas, and so forth, displayed in conjunction with books, help students choose good books. A variety of books should be available in a classroom library, with featured books changing every two weeks or so. A card in each book could contain the names of the students who have read the book, with room for comments by students. Because we acknowledge three purposes for reading, novels and story-books should comprise just a portion of the reading material available to students. Nonfiction books, including biographies, expository texts, magazines, newspapers, "how to" books and pamphlets, reference materials, and maps should also be available. Teachers should survey students to determine topics and activities that most interest them. Students will be motivated to read material that matches their curiosities, that relates to their prior knowledge and experiences, and that may be presented in some form other than traditional books.

Having special places in the classroom for reading will reinforce students' positive impression that reading is a valued and valuable endeavor. Reading lofts, couches, reading corners with lamps, and large throw pillows for "floor sitters" are just a few ideas for making reading inviting in a literature-rich classroom.

When possible allow students to make choices about the books they read. For class work purposes there will be parameters for what is read and by whom, but for leisure reading it is important to consider the following:

- Have a variety of reading material (books, magazines, newspapers, comic books, technical manuals).

- Never require a student to finish something if interest wanes.

- Do not always require formal accountability (test, book report, etc.). Instead, group and regroup students weekly to talk to each other about what they have read, or plan to read.

- Engage students in conversation about what they are reading.

- Share what you are reading.

- Talk often about the reasons for reading—pleasure or literacy experiences, information, task performance.

There is an abundance of quality books written for curious young minds. A literature-rich classroom should contain as many of the following Newbery Medal and Caldecott Award winning books as possible.

# Newbery Medal

1999   *Holes.* Louis Sachar
1998   *Out of the Dust.* Karen Hesse
1997   *The View from Saturday.* E.L. Konigsburg
1996   *Midwife's Apprentice.* Karen Cushman
1995   *Walk Two Moons.* Sharon Creech
1994   *The Giver.* Lois Lowry
1993   *Missing May.* Cynthia Rylant
1992   *Shiloh.* Phyllis Reynolds
1991   *Maniac Magee.* Jerry Spinellli
1990   *Number the Stars.* Lois Lowry
1989   *Joyful Noise.* Paul Fleischman
1988   *Lincoln: A Photobiography.* Russell Freedman
1987   *The Whipping Boy.* Sid Fleischman
1986   *Sarah, Plain and Tall.* Patricia MacLachlan
1985   *The Hero and the Crown.* Robin McKinley
1984   *Dear Mr. Henshaw.* Beverly Cleary
1983   *Dicey's Song.* Cynthia Voigt
1982   *A Visit to William Blake's Inn.* Nancy Willard
1981   *Jacob Have I Loved.* Katherine Paterson
1980   *A Gathering of Days.* Joan W. Blos
1979   *The Westing Game.* Ellen Raskin
1978   *Bridge to Terabithia.* Katherine Paterson
1977   *Roll of Thunder, Hear My Cry.* Mildred D. Taylor
1976   *The Grey King.* Susan Cooper
1975   *M.C. Higgins, the Great.* Virginia Hamilton
1974   *The Slave Dancer.* Paula Fox
1973   *Julie of the Wolves.* Jean George
1972   *Mrs. Frisby and the Rats of NIMH.* Robert C. O'Brien
1971   *Summer of the Swans.* Betsy Byars
1970   *Sounder.* William H. Armstrong
1969   *The High King.* Lloyd Alexander
1968   *From the Mixed-Up Files of Mrs. Basil E. Frankweiler.* E.L. Koningsburg
1967   *Up a Road Slowly.* Irene Hunt
1966   *I, Juan de Pareja.* Elizabeth Borton de Trevino
1965   *Shadow of a Bull.* Maia Wojciechowska
1964   *It's Like This, Cat.* Emily C. Neville
1963   *A Wrinkle in Time.* Madeline L'Engle
1962   *The Bronze Bow.* Elizabeth C. Speare
1961   *Island of the Blue Dolphins.* Scott O'Dell
1960   *Onion John.* Joseph Krumgold

# Caldecott Medal

1999   *Snowflake Bentley*. Jacqueline B. Martin
1998   *Rapunzel*. Paul O. Zelinsky
1997   *Golem*. David Wishiewski
1996   *Officer Buckle and Gloria*. P. Rathmann
1995   *Smoky Night*. David Diaz
1994   *Grandfather's Journey*. Allen Say
1993   *Mirette on the High Wire*. Emily A. McCully
1992   *Tuesday*. David Wiesner
1991   *Black and White*. David Macauley
1990   *Lon Po Po*. Ed Young
1989   *Song and Dance Man*. Stephen Gammell
1988   *Owl Moon*. John Schoenherr
1987   *Hey, Al*. Richard Egielski
1986   *The Polar Express*. Chris Van Allsburg
1985   *Saint George and the Dragon*. Trina Schart Hyman
1984   *The Glorious Flight: Across the Channel with Louis Bleriot*. Alice and Martin Provenson
1983   *Shadow*. Marcia Brown
1982   *Jumanji*. Chris Van Allsburg
1981   *Fables*. Arnold Lobel
1980   *Ox-Cart Man*. Barbara Cooney
1979   *The Girl Who Loved Wild Horses*. Paul Goble
1978   *Noah's Ark*. Peter Spier
1977   *Ashanti to Zulu: African Traditions*. Leo and Diane Dillon
1976   *Why Mosquitoes Buzz in People's Ears*. Leo and Diane Dillon
1975   *Arrow to the Sun: A Pueblo Indian Tale*. Gerald McDermott
1974   *Duffy and the Devil*. Margot Zemach
1973   *The Funny Little Woman*. Blair Lent
1972   *One Fine Day*. Nonny Hogrogian
1971   *A Story, A Story*. Gail E. Haley
1970   *Sylvester and the Magic Pebble*. William Steig
1969   *The Fool of the World and the Flying Ship*. Uri Shulevitz
1968   *Drummer Hoff*. Ed Emberly
1967   *Sam, Bangs and Moonshine*. Evaline Ness
1966   *Always Room for One More*. Nonny Hogrogian
1965   *May I Bring a Friend?* Beni Montresor
1964   *Where the Wild Things Are*. Maurice Sendak
1963   *The Snowy Day*. Ezra Jack Keats
1962   *Once a Mouse*. Marcia Brown
1961   *Baboushka and the Three Kings*. Nicholas Sidjakov
1960   *Nine Days to Christmas*. Marie Hall Ets

## Be a Reading Role Model

Students watch us even when they pretend to not care and would never admit that they admire us. So be a reading role model! During designated reading times, it is tempting to grade papers or catch up on administrative work. Don't give in! Read while the students read. Read a variety of materials, but always have a novel that you go back to when time permits. Ask students about what they are reading as you walk down the hall or wait for the bus or eat lunch. Have frequent conversations about what you are reading, or plan to read, as soon as you finish your current book. Talk to students about information you gain from reading.

# Explicitly Teach Reading Comprehension

Most widely used standardized tests require students to read a passage and then answer questions. The passages may be narrative fiction or nonfiction, in the form of letters, memos, friendly notes, and so on. The questions accompanying reading passages require students to analyze what they read to determine a wide range of information. Here is a list of some, but not nearly all, of the reading strategies covered by the test questions. Making a giant-size poster of these areas will allow you and your students to refer to them in class discussions. Explicitly teach these strategies through mini-lessons and guided practice.

—determining the main idea
—differentiating between fact and fiction
—understanding the author's purpose
—using a story web
—sequencing events
—choosing the best title
—comparing and contrasting
—making inferences
—making predictions
—recognizing extraneous information
—identifying reading strategies

—defining vocabulary within context
—identifying pertinent details
—identifying connections
—understanding characters
—identifying setting
—understanding plot
—generalizing through analogies
—interpreting figures of speech
—drawing conclusions
—extending meaning

While not all of these areas will be a part of the questions accompanying each reading passage, we can be sure that most or all of them will appear within the complete reading battery of TerraNova, Metropolitan Achievement Test, California Achievement Test, California Test of Basic Skills, Iowa Test of Basic Skills, and Stanford Achievement Test.

"Understanding the question is half the solution." What an appropriate adage when it comes to answering questions about reading passages. Helping students understand what is being asked enables them to select and write the correct answer. Because visual learning is so important, as is connecting instruction to actual practice, a chart/poster of the areas of information likely to be tested (see pg. 57) will serve as a reminder of all the various components of writing and a handy reference guide for teachers and students.

On almost every standardized test, reading comprehension is assessed in the format of a reading passage followed by questions pertaining to it. There are two kinds of questions used. One format calls for students to choose a correct answer from among four or five choices. These are called *Selected Response Items*. The other format asks students to write an answer to a question or prompt. These are called *Constructed Response Items*. The trend in standardized testing is toward *Constructed Response Items*. Both formats are used in the student practices sections that follow. There are many books published solely to provide reading comprehension practice. Passages followed by both Selected Response Items and Constructed Response Items should be used regularly to give students opportunities to practice their skills and to practice their comfort level with testing formats. The reading comprehension student practice pages that follow are written for either grades 4 and 5 or grades 6, 7, 8.

# Teacher-Directed Practice for Grades 4 and 5

The following is an example of a teacher-directed class discussion. Such a discussion should follow the reading of a passage, first silently and then aloud. Put this passage and the three questions on page 45 on an overhead transparency.

> Anderson Abbott was the first Canadian-born black doctor. Born in 1837, he began practicing medicine when he was only twenty-three. When the Civil War broke out in the United States in 1861, Dr. Abbott decided that his skills were needed by the Union Army. He served as one of only eight black surgeons in the Civil War. In 1863 he was placed in charge of all the army hospitals in Washington, D.C., where he stayed until the war ended.

> Dr. Abbott went back to Canada after the war. He began writing articles in newspapers and he became the president of the Chatham Library and Debate Society. The United States honored him by giving him a *shawl* worn by President Abraham Lincoln. Dr. Abbott died in 1913.

"Now that we have read the passage, let's begin with the first question."

**Questions:**

**1.** *Dr. Abbott is important in history mainly because...*

"Before we even look at the choices, where would we put this item on our chart? (Wait for several responses.) Actually, I can see it fitting several places, but the one that seems best is *drawing conclusions*. We are given a lot of information about Dr. Abbott and now it is up to us to decide the main reason he is important in history. Let's look at our choices."

A. *he was president of the Chatham Library and Debate Society*

"After reading about Dr. Abbott, does being president of a library seem very important? (Wait) No, I don't think so either; let's cross it out. How about B?"

B. *he wore a shawl owned by President Lincoln*

"Does it say he actually wore the shawl? No, so that's not it. [cross it out] Now to C."

C. *he was so young when he became a doctor*

"This one stands out as unusual. Even in modern times, twenty-three is very young to be a doctor. But when we look at D, it becomes obvious that being a black doctor in the Civil War is more unusual than being young. So the answer is D."

D. *he was a black surgeon in the Civil War*

"Let's go on to question 2."

**2.** *Where was Dr. Abbott born?*

"What kind of question is this? (Wait) Yes, it's asking for pertinent details. I've always thought of this as the easiest kind of question. After all, the answers are right in front of us! Without even looking at the choices, who can tell me where Dr. Abbott was born? (Wait) Yes! Canada! Now, look at the choices and tell me which answer is correct." (All should quickly respond "D".)

A. Chatham
B. United States
C. Washington, D.C.
D. Canada

"Now to question 3."

**3.** *In the passage, the word* shawl *refers to a small, light, woven blanket worn over the shoulders to take off the chill. Who wore the shawl given to Dr. Abbott? _____*

"What are we looking for here? (Wait) Yes, I agree, it's very much like #2. We are looking for detail. This time, however, there will be no choices. (Quickly reveal the blank space under #3.) We have to come up with an answer. Look for the word *shawl* in the passage. Now tell me who wore it! Yes, easy, isn't it?"

This kind of teacher-student dialogue should be repeated periodically, with opportunities for independent practice in between.

Independent Practice 1—Grades 4, 5

# Reading Comprehension

Student
Page

As I went along, I could not help but think back to the happy days with Father and Mother in Nanam, Korea. We lived in a beautiful big house with many different-sized tatami-mat rooms. Our home was surrounded by a graceful bamboo grove. My stomach was always filled with good food. I had plenty of clothes to wear and several pairs of fine shoes.

However, just before midnight on July 29, 1945, Mother, Ko, and I had to flee. We had learned from a friend in the Japanese Army, Corporal Matsumua, that the Communists were about to attack our town. Father was away in Manchuria, and Hideyo was working in an ammunition factory twenty miles from home. We left Father and Hideyo a note asking them to meet us at the train station in Seoul. While we were fleeing for safety in the South, an airplane dropped a bomb and I was thrown into the air. This incident left me deaf in my right ear, and also with constant back pain. Until we reached Seoul, we lived on leaves from bushes and what Ko found on Korean farmland. When we arrived in Seoul, we learned that atom bombs had been dropped on Nagasaki and Hiroshima, and that Japan had lost World War II. The Korean peninsula was divided in half and the Communists had taken over the North. We could never go back to our home in the bamboo grove. We had become refugees.

**1.** Who is the main character?
   A. Mother
   B. the narrator
   C. Father
   D. Hideyo

**2.** Where is the setting of the story? _____

   Did the Communists take over this city at the end of World War II? _____
   (yes or no)

**3.** How did the narrator become deaf in one ear?
   A. from the Japanese Army
   B. from a bomb dropped by an airplane
   C. from eating bushes and leaves
   D. from being dropped as a baby

**Independent Practice 1—Grades 4, 5**

# Reading Comprehension (Cont.)

Student
Page

**4.** Why couldn't the family return home? _____

**5.** Where is the end of the story set? _____

Is this city in North or South Korea? _____

**6.** What happens to the characters in the story?
   A. They join the army.
   B. They become rich and famous.
   C. They find Hideyo.
   D. They become refugees.

**7.** In the story, what does the word *refugee* mean?
   A. someone who has gotten lost
   B. someone forced from his homeland or who leaves because of danger
   C. a person who is poor
   D. a child whose family decides to move to another town

**Independent Practice 2—Grades 4, 5**

# Reading Comprehension

The following afternoon Miguel Torres took the helm and steered the ponga homeward. As the boat skimmed past the rock reef, Miguel's brother, Tomas, stood on the bow and looked down at the red-orange sea, which now reflected the colors of the sunset. He saw nothing larger than a parrot fish.

The ponga shot out of the cove and into the Shallows, which lay between the island and the peninsula. The water was only about fifty feet deep. Many sharks came here to give birth to their live young or to lay eggs, as some do. Into these protected waters also came old and ill sharks. They could slow their continuous swimming by heading into the currents and letting the swiftly flowing water rush through their gills. They used less energy this way and could rest and heal themselves. And into these waters came the Torres men to maintain their reputation as Loreta's best shark fishermen. The Shallows were sometimes called the Torres.

**1.** What is the *ponga?* _____

**2.** The Shallows is between the _____ and the _____ .

**3.** What characters appear in this section? _____

_____

**4.** About how deep is the water in the Shallows? _____

**5.** Why did the Torres men go into these waters? _____

_____

**6.** What other name did people give to the Shallows? _____

**7.** Why do you think they called it that? _____

_____

From *Be a Super Test-Taker*, Level E-F (24-25), Scholastic, Inc. 1995.

# Teacher-Directed Practice for Grades 6, 7, and 8

The following is an example of a teacher-directed class discussion. Use it as a guideline for your own discussion. Put the passage and three questions on an overhead transparency. Have the class read the passage silently, and then read it aloud.

Following World War II, the nations of the world wanted to make sure that nothing so terrible would ever happen again. They formed an organization called the United Nations. It was, and still is today, a place where leaders of nations could talk about their disagreements and work out a peaceful *resolution* to problems.

During the 1950s, the man who served as the Secretary General of the United States was Dag Hammerskjold. He was known as a peacemaker in the disputes in the Middle East, Egypt, and Israel. Many of the world's problems centered on the Suez Canal, the waterway between Africa and Europe.

The membership of the U.N. grew rapidly to over one hundred countries. Many of the sessions were less than peaceful. There were heated disagreements as Hammerskjold tried to persuade nations to work out their differences without violence. Because the members respected him for his fairness, Hammerskjold was able to keep peaceful relationships as nations solved their problems.

But in 1960, a civil war in the Congo threatened to cause war all over Africa. Hammerskjold decided to go to the Congo to see if he could help. On his way to the Congo he died in a plane crash in the jungle in 1963. The whole world mourned.

"Now that we have read the passage, let's begin with the first question..."

Questions:

1. Which event belongs between the two in the chart in chronological order?
   *United Nations formed* >_____ > *Major problems in the Suez Canal*

   A. Civil war in the Congo
   B. Hammerskjold elected U.N. Secretary General
   C. U.N. membership grew to one hundred
   D. Hammerskjold dies in plane crash

"Take a look at the chart and decide what kind of item this is. Who can tell us? (Wait) That's right! We are asked to sequence events. Can we do this by simply reading a paragraph? (Wait) No, it takes an overview of the whole passage. Since we already read the whole passage, let's go back and scan for the first event, *United Nations formed*. Do you see it? Would someone come up and point to it? Thank you. I'm going to mark it lightly." (Put dot by the third line.)

"Now let's scan for *Suez Canal*."
(Repeat as with United Nations.)

"Okay. Let's see what happened between the formation of the United Nations and problems in the Suez Canal. I see the name *Dag Hammerskjold* between our two dots. Look at choices B and D. Does it make sense that B comes before D? Of course! So B is the correct answer.
We need to be careful to not answer sequencing questions too quickly. Sometimes they can be tricky.

Now let's go to the next item."

   **2.** *In the passage, what does the word* resolution *mean?* _____

"The first thing we need to do is find the word. Would someone please come up and point to it for us?... Thank you. (Put a dot by the fourth line.) Would someone please read the sentence containing the word *resolution*? (student reads) Does *resolution* sound like a good or bad thing? (Wait for responses.) I agree! If people are 'talking' and they work out something 'peacefully,' then *resolution* is good. In fact, it sounds like an *answer* or a *solution*. (Write the word *solution* on the board.) Hey, what word does this look like? (Wait) Right! It looks a lot like *resolution*. So who would like to tell us a definition of *resolution*?" (Allow for several students to answer. Then ask students to help put the thoughts together to make one brief answer.)

"Let's go to the next question."

   **3.** *The author's main purpose in writing this article is to...*
       A. inform us about a famous man.
       B. give us details about the formation of the U.N.
       C. tell us the reasons for the civil war in the Congo.
       D. warn us not to fly over the jungle in a plane.

"Take a look at the chart. What kind of item is this? (Wait) Right! It is 'understanding author's purpose.' Can we do that by reading only one paragraph? (Wait) Can we do that by quickly scanning? (Wait) What do we need to do to determine the author's main purpose? (Wait) Yes! We have to carefully read the whole passage. In this item we don't need to write the author's main purpose. We are given four choices. Let's look at them one at a time." (Reveal choices one at a time.)

   A. *inform us about a famous man*

"Who would that famous man be? (Wait) That's right, it's *Dag Hammerskjold*. By the way, have you noticed how unusual his last name is? Let's all say it together. (Say it as a class several times.) So the passage tells us a lot about Dag Hammerskjold...Even though that's true, one of the other choices might be better. Never answer an 'understanding author's purpose' or a 'main idea' question before considering all the choices. Let's go on to B."

   B. *give us details about the formation of the U.N.*
"What facts are we given about the U.N.? (Wait for students to name: *formation, Hammerskjold as Secretary General, membership grew*.) Anything else? (Wait) So what do we know more about from the passage, Dag Hammerskjold or the U.N.? (Wait) I agree! There is more about Dag Hammerskjold. Well, let's go on to C."

   C. *tell us the reasons for the civil war in the Congo*

"Where do we first read about the Congo? (Wait) Yes, not until the last paragraph. So that's not the best choice. Our last choice is D."

> D. *warn us not to fly over the jungle in a plane*

"Like C, choice D is only mentioned in the last paragraph. It looks like our best choice is A!"

This kind of teacher-student dialogue should be repeated periodically, with opportunities for independent practice in between.

Independent Practice 1—Grades 6, 7, 8

# Reading Comprehension

Student Page

Dear Mayor Roberts,

In our seventh-grade social studies class we have been studying politics. We have learned about national, state, and local government. As we have discussed community leaders and how decisions are made, we have thought of a few questions we want to ask you.

Why don't you have teenagers on the City Council? We have opinions and suggestions that could help our city. If you are able to appoint the Council, would you consider asking a teenager to serve?

Last April the city imposed a curfew for teenagers sixteen and under. We don't understand why we have to be off the streets by 10:00 P.M. on weeknights. Did the City Council receive that many complaints about things that teenagers do at night? Did you think about asking parents for their opinions? Did anyone talk to teenagers before the decision was made?

The City Council announced last week that Main Street will be changed to Eugene Green Boulevard next month. We know that Dr. Green has given a lot to our city for many years, but there are other people who have dedicated themselves to making our lives better. How was Dr. Green chosen to be honored this way? Did anyone ask teenagers who they think deserves a street named after them?

When you have time, please help us understand how decisions are made at the city level by answering our questions. Could you come and speak to our class sometime? Thank you for the good work you do for our city.

Sincerely,
Joseph Plotter
Student Representative
Mrs. Johnson's Class
Wilson Middle School

**Questions:**

1. What do the students most want the mayor to do? _____

_____

_____

_____

Independent Practice 1—Grades 6, 7, 8

# Reading Comprehension (Cont.)

2. Does the letter writer understand why there is a curfew? Yes _____ No _____

How do you know? _____

_____

_____

3. Is the letter writer hostile towards the mayor? Yes _____ No _____

Defend your opinion. _____

_____

_____

4. Which is not a main issue addressed in the letter?
   A. teenagers on City Council
   B. teenage curfew
   C. parents on City Council
   D. renaming Main Street

5. Do you think that the mayor will be impressed with Mrs. Johnson's social

   studies class when he visits? Yes _____ No _____ Why or why not?

_____

_____

6. Who does the letter writer think the City Council should have asked before they
   decided on the new name for Main Street?
   A. the mayor
   B. teenagers
   C. Mrs. Johnson's social studies class
   D. parents

Independent Practice 2—Grades 6, 7, 8

# Reading Comprehension

**Student Page**

In the 1800s, Impressionism was a very popular style of painting in Europe. Impressionist painters tried to make their pictures realistic rather than *posed*. They wanted to depict nature as it is. At this time in history, almost all famous painters were men. The world did not expect women to be artists until one woman, Mary Cassatt, changed this *misconception*. She was determined to show her talent. She left Pennsylvania and moved to France to study Impressionist painting.

Mary Cassatt loved to paint mothers and their children in Impressionistic style. She painted very pleasant, happy pictures using pastel colors. Her paintings often contained bright, sunny rooms with children playing and mothers watching with smiling faces.

As talented as she was, her beautiful paintings were not recognized as important or valuable until after she died. In fact, Mary Cassatt never sold a picture. But today she is considered one of the most famous American artists. Her paintings hang in museums around the world.

**Questions:**

**1.** Which of the following is an *opinion*?
    A. Mary Cassatt enjoyed painting children.
    B. Impressionism was a popular form of art in the 1800s.
    C. Mary Cassatt became famous after her death.
    D. Mary Cassatt was a better painter than most men during her lifetime.

**2.** In the passage, the word *posed* refers to...
    A. paintings kept in safe places
    B. planned rather than occurring naturally
    C. sold to museums
    D. a position of power

**3.** The word *misconception* in the passage means _____

_____

**4.** Mary Cassatt left Pennsylvania because she had a desire to _____

_____

_____

# Reading Comprehension

Mama took my arm and pulled me up. "Over here, Cassie," she said, directing me to a chair next to the fireplace and behind Big Ma, who was ironing our clothes for the next day.

I peeped around Big Ma's long skirts and saw Mama guiding Stacey to her own desk. Then back she went for Little Man and, picking him up bodily, set him in the chair beside her rocker. Christopher-John she left alone at the study table. Then she gathered all our study materials and brought them to us with a look that said she would *tolerate* no more of this foolishness.

With Big Ma before me, I could see nothing else and I grew serious enough to complete my arithmetic assignment. When that was finished, I lingered before opening my reader, watching Big Ma as she ironed my dress, then placed her heavy iron on a small pile of embers in a corner of the fireplace and picked up a second iron warming there. She tested the iron with a tap of her finger and put it back again.

While Big Ma waited for the iron to get hot, I could see Mama bending over outspread newspapers scraping the dried mud off the old field shoes of Papa's which she wore daily, stuffed with wads of newspaper, over her own shoes to protect them from the mud and rain. Little Man beside her was deep into his first-grade reader, his eyebrows *furrowed* in concentration. Ever since Mama had brought the reader home with the offensive inside cover no longer visible, Little Man had accepted the book as a necessity for passing the first grade. But he took no pride in it. Looking up, he noticed that Big Ma was preparing to iron his clothes, and he smiled happily. Then his eyes met mine and silent laughter creased his face. I muffled a giggle and Mama looked up.

"Cassie, you start up again and I'm sending you to the kitchen to study," she warned.

"Yes'm," I said, settling back in my chair and beginning to read. I certainly did not want to go to the kitchen. Now that the fire no longer burned in the stove, it was cold in there.

Independent Practice 3—Grades 6, 7, 8

# Reading Comprehension (Cont.)

Student
Page

## Questions:

**1.** In the passage, "silent laughter" refers to:
    A. putting your hand over your mouth when you laugh
    B. turning down the volume of your TV
    C. laughter that no one is around to hear
    D. inner enjoyment

**2.** Why didn't the speaker want to go back to the kitchen? _____

_____

**3.** How did Big Mama heat her iron?
    A. by plugging it into the electric socket
    B. by leaving it out in the sun
    C. by putting it on the fire embers
    D. by immersing it in boiling water

**4.** What was Big Mama's opinion of doing schoolwork?
    A. She thought it was boring.
    B. She didn't encourage children to spend time studying.
    C. She spent much of her day reading.
    D. She appears to value education.

**5.** In the passage, the word *tolerate* refers to
    A. acceptance
    B. disobedience
    C. a kind of laughter
    D. denial

**6.** What does Big Mama put in Papa's field shoes? _____

Why does she do this? _____

_____

_____

• From *Roll of Thunder, Hear My Cry* by Mildred D. Taylor (Penguin Books, 1977).

# READING COMPREHENSION

# Strategy Suggestions

**Student Page**

**1** Remember that reading comprehension involves A WIDE RANGE OF SKILLS:

-determining main idea
-differentiating between fact
  and opinion
-understanding author's purpose
-using a story web
-sequencing events
-choosing best title
-comparing and contrasting
-making inferences
-making predictions
-recognizing extraneous
  information

-defining vocabulary within context
-identifying pertinent details
-identifying reading strategies
-identifying connections
-understanding characters
-identifying setting
-understanding plot
-generalizing through analogies
-interpreting figures of speech
-drawing conclusions
-extending meaning

**2** When you have a passage to read followed by questions, READ THE QUESTIONS FIRST. This will give you a good idea of what to look for as you read the passage.

**3** When you are asked to choose a definition for a word in the passage, the word will usually be italicized. SCAN THE PASSAGE to find the word. Reading the sentence before, the sentence containing the word, and the sentence following the word will usually give you enough information to answer the question correctly. Without reading the word in context, you might choose a definition that is accurate for the word, but not the one that fits the passage.

**4** Always LOOK BACK AT THE PASSAGE to answer questions rather than relying on memory.

# Strategy Suggestions (Cont.)

**Student Page**

**5** Look for key words such as *first, then, next, finally* and *after* when sequencing events.

**6** Always READ ALL THE CHOICES before answering a question.

**7** Look for NEGATIVE WORDS in questions. These include phrases such as "What is the opposite of...", "Which one is not included...", "All of these happened except...", etc.

**8** The MAIN IDEA of a passage is most often at the very beginning and it may be stated again at the very end.

**9** If you are asked about CAUSE AND EFFECT, look for key words such as *since, because, as a result of,* and *therefore.*

**10** Don't be discouraged by VERY LONG PASSAGES. Most tests contain a long passage and then a short one. It's okay to answer questions about the short ones first as long as you are careful to put answers with the right item numbers.

# CHAPTER 4

# Language Arts Mechanics

The format used for testing language arts skills on standardized tests varies both among tests and, from year to year, within individual tests. The skills tested vary much less than the format. When a state, district, or school chooses a particular test and orders accompanying testing information, format samples are available. Classroom teachers can access format samples through their test coordinators at whatever level the decision process takes place. If a test preparation book such as this one is published in 2000, the formats given may change in 2001 with new published editions of the standardized tests. It should be understood that references to standardized tests indicated for any format are tentative. A format may be used in grades 4 and 5 for a particular test, but not used in grades 6,7, 8. A format used in one edition may not be used in previous or forthcoming editions. Teachers should stay in touch on a regular basis with their testing coordinator to remain current.

The wisdom to be gained by understanding the variability of the testing formats is that fostering the *flexibility* of students should be a primary classroom goal. Teachers know that often students actually have the knowledge and skills that are tested, but they can so easily appear to not have them because of their unfamiliarity with the way test items are presented. This is especially true in language arts mechanics and expression.

In this chapter the skills tested on the major standardized tests will be presented in a variety of formats. If you decide to lean heavily toward a particular format that you know will be a part of the coming test, that's fine, but to increase flexibility and give students practice in showing what they know, they should be exposed to knowledge and skills tested in a variety of ways. This will help them on the tests, as they will be practiced at adapting their knowledge to new formats.

To practice spelling and reading comprehension, it is necessary for practice exercises to contain grade-level-specific vocabulary and comprehension skills. However, practicing mechanics and expression skills is possible even if the vocabulary and sentence structure used are not written specifically for a grade level. In other words, both fourth graders and eighth graders can practice capitalization, punctuation, verb tense, proper pronouns, topic sentence identification, etc., using material written for students in grades 4, 5, 6, 7 or 8. The knowledge and skills tested are not dependent on the level of difficulty of the context.

# Capitalization: Sample Formats with Test-Wise Strategies to Share with Students

Here are some sample formats commonly used on the indicated standardized tests, along with comments that may be helpful when instructing on the skill.

## The test: CAT, CTBS • The skill: Recognizing Errors

Put the following paragraph on a transparency.

**Directions:** Look for the part of the sentence that contains a word that should begin with a capital letter. If all the words are correctly written, choose "none."

I will openly admit / that San francisco / is a city I have / always wanted to visit.  none
A                 B               C               D             E

**The strategy:** Students should read the entire sentence before searching for errors. There are times when an error will leap off the page during the initial reading. Even so, direct students to go back and look carefully at each phrase to either check their initial response or detect errors.

## The test: ITBS • The skill: Recognizing Errors

**Directions:** Choose the line that has a capitalization error. If there are no capitalization errors, choose "no mistakes."

    (1)  The beagle is a            (3)  They are often named snoop.y
    (2)  lovable breed of dog.     (4)  no mistakes

**The strategy:** Many students find the numbers distracting. It helps them to cover the numbers with their index finger or a piece of scratch paper. When a mistake is identified, the finger or paper is removed and then the number beside the line with the mistake is bubbled in.

## The test: SAT • The skill: Choosing Correct Phrases

Rather than simply recognizing errors, this format requires students to choose the correct phrase from among four phrases with the same words, but varied capitalization.

**Directions:** Choose the word or words that is capitalized correctly to complete each sentence.

    My teacher read a poem called _____.
    (A)  "and then They were gone."     (C)  "and then They Were Gone."
    (B)  "And Then They Were Gone."    (D)  "and then they were gone."

**The strategy:** If students simply look at the four choices and bubble in answers based on assumptions and not on context, many mistakes are possible. In this sample, "and then they were gone" could be part of dialogue, or any ordinary phrase, if the quotation marks are ignored. However, when read in context it is obvious that capital letters are required because the phrase is actually the title of a poem. The context should be emphasized for every format.

# When to Use **Capital Letters**

**Student Page**

Mistakes in capitalization are easy to miss. When we read quickly, we often concentrate so hard on context that we overlook simple capitalization errors. Here is a list of some uses for capital letters:

Capitalize proper names
* ★ Names of people (first, last, initials)
    * Bob
    * Mr. Wilson
    * Jesse D. White

* ★ Names of places and nationalities
    * Africa
    * Boston
    * Australian
    * Elm Street
    * Rocky Mountains
    * Mississippi River
    * Chesapeake Bay
    * European

* ★ Names of political and religious groups
    * Republican
    * Baptists

Capitalize the proper pronoun I

Capitalize official titles when used with names
* ★ Mayor Riley
* ★ Mrs. White
* ★ Senator Thurmond

Capitalize first letter in first word of a sentence or quote
* ★ We will do that later.
* ★ His brother yelled, "Don't go near the edge!"

Capitalize greetings and closings of letters
* ★ Dear Linda,
* ★ Sincerely yours,
* ★ With love,
* ★ Greetings all!

Capitalize the names of days, months, and holidays
* ★ Monday
* ★ August
* ★ Thanksgiving

Name _____    Date _____

Capitalization: Grades 4–8/Independent Practice 1

# Identifying Mistakes

**Directions:** Look for the part of the sentence that contains a word that should begin with a capital letter. If all the words are correctly written, choose "none."

**Sample:**

Next semester / we will all read / Island of the blue dolphin / in class.   none
   A            B            C          D    E

a few days ago / I decided / to do all my / shopping Tuesday.   none
   F            G            H          I       J

The main words in titles of books and stories and poems begin with capital letters. Part C is the title of a book so blue dolphin should be Blue Dolphin.
The beginning letter of the first word in a sentence should be capitalized. So in Part F, a should be A.

1. When we told Mike / he could come, / he shouted / "oh, good!"   none
     A           B           C         D     E

2. The state / of Texas shares / a border with / Mexico.   none
    F           G           H         I     J

3. We walked / around the town / with mr. Edwards, / our teacher.   none
    A            B             C         D     E

4. The last word / in the spelling bee / was correctly spelled / by shelly.   none
    F           G              H         I     J

5. If you can / study on saturday / I will change / my weekend plans.   none
    A           B           C         D     E

6. My sister / Sandy and i / like to play / soccer at the local field.   none
    F           G           H         I     J

7. Paul / recently visited / Daytona beach, Florida / to go ocean fishing.   none
    A        B           C         D     E

8. "Have you ever seen / a better / Disney movie?" / Angela asked Matt.   none
    F           G           H         I     J

Capitalization: Grades 4–8/Independent Practice 2

# Identifying Mistakes

**Directions:** Choose the line that has a capitalization error. If there are no capitalization errors, choose "No mistakes."

**Sample:**

A  My grandmother lives in
B  the yellow house on Elm
C  Street in Waco, Texas.
D  No mistakes

If reading through this for the first time doesn't show errors, go over it again one line at a time. Writing "My grandmother" is different from calling her "Grandmother" without the word my. In line A, grandmother is NOT capitalized. Elm Street is a proper name and so is Waco, Texas. There are no mistakes in this sample, so choice D is correct.

E  I will be going to camp for the
F  last time next summer.  I
G  will be a Counselor then.
H  No mistakes

In line E, the word *camp* is fine as it is. If it were followed by a name, then *camp* and the name would be capitalized. In line G the word *Counselor* should be *counselor*. It's the same as saying "I will be a cook" or "a student" or "a friend." Choice G is correct.

I. A  The sixth-grade History teacher
   B  at Milburn Middle School has
   C  taught for more than fifteen years.
   D  No mistakes

2. E  "Hurry!" yelled my dad.
   F  "we will be late for the
   G  opening ceremony."
   H  No mistakes

3. A  John's favorite holiday is
   B  thanksgiving.  He likes to
   C  eat a big dinner with his family.
   D  No mistakes

4. E  As a child, one of my favorite
   F  stories was "Snow White
   G  and the seven dwarfs."
   H  No mistakes

5. A  After a spring rain the mountains
   B  seem to glisten with freshness
   C  as the water coats the new grass.
   D  No mistakes

6. E  Mr. Hill teaches arts and
   F  crafts every summer at the
   G  camp on lake Munroe.
   H  No mistakes

7. A  My Aunt Amy and Uncle Ted
   B  grow corn. They own many acres
   C  of farmland in georgia.
   D  No mistakes

8. E  Jim shouted to his brother, "look
   F  out for the dog running down the
   G  hill behind you!"
   H  No mistakes

**Independent Practice**

# Filling in the Blank

**Directions:** Choose the word or group of words that is capitalized correctly to complete each sentence.

**Sample:**

The holiday fair will open on _____ .
- A  Sunday, December 12
- B  Sunday, december 12
- C  sunday, December 12
- D  sunday, december 12

Proper nouns like days of the week and months should begin with capital letters. Line A is correct because both *Sunday* and *December* are correct.

The coach said, _____ .
- A  "Put up the Lawn equipment."
- B  "put up the lawn Equipment."
- C  "put up the lawn equipment."
- D  "Put up the lawn equipment."

The first word in a direct quote should be capitalized. So *put* should be *Put*. The words *lawn equipment* should not be capitalized because neither is a proper noun. Choice D is correct.

1. We may never be able to count all the stars in the _____ .
- E  Milky Way
- F  milky Way
- G  Milky way
- H  milky way

2. Janet's vacation was to _____ .
- A  New england
- B  New England
- C  new england
- D  new England

3. Our teacher read a story called _____
- E  "It Wasn't Enough."
- F  "it wasn't enough."
- G  "It Wasn't enough."
- H  "It wasn't Enough."

**Independent Practice**

# Filling in the Blank (Cont.)

**4.** My cousin is from _____ .

      A  west virginia

      B  West Virginia

      C  west Virginia

      D  West virginia

**5.** This article was in the _____ .

      E  Post and courier

      F  post and courier

      G  post and Courier

      H  Post and Courier

**6.** The Great Gatsby was written by _____ .

      A  F. scott fitzgerald

      B  f. scott Fitzgerald

      C  F. Scott Fitzgerald

      D  f. scott fitzgerald

**7.** To travel to Texas she must go _____ .

      E  South, then East

      F  south, then East

      G  South, then east

      H  south, then east

**8.** They saw many replicas at the _____ .

      A  Brooklyn Museum

      B  Brooklyn museum

      C  brooklyn museum

      D  brooklyn Museum

# Punctuation: Sample Formats with Test-Wise Strategies to Share with Students

Here are some sample formats commonly used on the indicated standardized tests, along with comments that may be helpful when discussing a skill with your students.

## The test: CAT, CTBS • The skill: Identifying Missing Punctuation

**Directions:** Choose the punctuation mark that would make the sentence correct. If no other punctuation is needed, choose "none."

"The next time I see you we will talk, promised Ann.

    (A) .   (B) ;   (C) "   (D) ?   (E) none

**The strategy:** Students should look at the entire sentence to check for quotations, lists, etc. that will give them clues concerning missing punctuation.

## The test: CAT, CTBS • The skill: Choosing Correct Punctuation

**Directions:** Choose the correct punctuation for the underlined part of each sentence. If no other punctuation is needed, choose "correct as is."

<u>Aunt Millie our favorite aunt</u> said we could go.
(A)  Aunt Millie: our favorite aunt
(B)  Aunt Millie, our favorite aunt
(C)  Aunt Millie our favorite aunt,
(D)  Aunt Millie, our favorite aunt,
(E)  correct as is

**The strategy:** Students should try each choice as a substitute for the underlined part of the sentence before making a choice.

## The test: ITBS • The skill: Identifying Errors

**Directions:** Choose the line with a punctuation error. Choose "no mistake" if there is no error.

(1)  We have two innings
(2)  left in the game.  Can
(3)  we score enough points to win.
(4)  no mistake

**The strategy:** As with capitalization, covering the numbers with an index finger or with scratch paper makes it easier for students to spot errors.

## The test: SAT • The skill: Choosing Correct Responses

**Directions:** Choose the line with a punctuation error. Choose "no mistake" if there is no error.

Mom sighed when she said _____

- (A)  , "Its been a long day."
- (B)  "It's been a long day"
- (C)  , "It's been a long day."
- (D)  "It's been a long day."
- (E)  no mistake

**The strategy:** Students need to silently read each choice option in context, not as separate phrases. In this sample (D) appears correct if the sentence is not considered. Within context, the comma before the phrase is necessary, making (C) the correct choice. Items such as these are complicated because they contain multiple punctuations.

LANGUAGE ARTS MECHANICS

# Punctuation Uses

Student Page

*A comma may be used...*

—to separate words in a series
  He had a ball, bat, and glove.

—between the day and year in a date
  February 27, 1999

—to separate a quotation from the rest of the sentence
  Jesse called, "Look out for that tree!"

—between a city and state
  Charleston, South Carolina

—after the greeting of a friendly letter
  Dear Cody,

—after the closing of most letters
  Love to all,

—before the conjunction in a compound sentence
  Travis went to work, and Noah went to the beach.

—to set off a person's name who is being addressed
  Rachel, I need help with the dishes.

—to set off beginning or introductory words
  Therefore, we changed our plans.

—to set off words of phrases or proper nouns that explain
  Snoopy, the cuter of the two dogs, barked at everything.

*A period may be used...*

—to end a sentence that is a statement
  The four boys decided to go surfing.

—to end abbreviations
  Mrs. White        Colonial Dr.
  Dr. Powell        The Mason Co.
  Tues., Feb. 2     Scholastic, Inc.

# Punctuation Uses (Cont.)

—after initials
V.S. Davis
W.J. Clinton

*An apostrophe may be used...*
—in possessive nouns or pronouns
car's muffler
table's legs
Sara's books
Woody's dish

—in contractions

| | |
|---|---|
| can't | I'll |
| won't | didn't |
| we're | we've |

*Quotation marks may be used...*
—to indicate spoken words
"We've come a long way today," remarked Rus.

—to indicate some titles (songs, poems, stories)
"Hey, Jude"
"Stopping by Woods on a Snowy Evening"
"The Jumping Frog"

*A semicolon may be used...*
—to separate two complete thoughts in the same sentence
The boys knew her name; they had simply forgotten her.

*A colon may be used...*
—to separate a list from the rest of the sentence
The lady had three daughters: Erin, Laura, and Maggie.

—after the greeting of a business letter
Dear Commander Powell:

# LANGUAGE ARTS MECHANICS ⌐ ▪ ⌐ ▪ ⌐ ▪ ⌐ ▪ ⌐ ▪ ⌐

**Punctuation Activity**

# Perilous Punctuation

This activity is designed for groups of three or four.

**Materials:** colored index cards or tag board cut to the size of cards (a different color for each group) pocket chart or bulletin board with tacks

**Activity:**

**1.** Students form groups of three or four.

**2.** Teacher gives each student at least six cards, with access to more. All the students in a group should get the same color card.

**3.** Individually, the students should write as many uses for a variety of punctuation marks as they can. Multiple uses of one punctuation are encouraged, but each use must go on a separate card. Allow about 15 minutes for this step.

**4.** Groups then get together to compare cards. If more than one person wrote the same punctuation use, then the group must decide which one is articulated best. For instance, Marcus and Alan both wrote about using commas to separate words in a series. The group thinks that Alan's is the easier to understand, so they choose to use his. They may rewrite the use on another card if they feel it is necessary. Allow about 10 minutes.

**5.** The groups now write a sentence for each different use with the punctuation mark eliminated. For the example in 4., the group's sentence might be:

*We went to the store to buy tuna melons bread and milk.* Allow about 15 minutes.

**6.** The groups now exchange pages of sentences with errors. They edit (*correct*) the pages and give them back so writing teams can check and approve or disapprove. Allow 15 minutes.

**7.** The teacher will facilitate a round-robin among the groups. Each group will read a use card and then place it back in the pocket chart or tack it on the bulletin board. Groups will take turns. Uses may not be repeated. The group posting the last use wins the game.

This becomes a student-generated, interactive board.

**Follow up:**

**1.** Take the cards from the board, shuffle them, and give each group (same or new groupings) an equal number of use cards.

**2.** Groups will write a friendly letter incorporating all the uses. This can serve as a group assignment.

—If the groups are told to leave out the appropriate punctuation, letters can be exchanged and groups may edit each other's.

—This process may be repeated using a variety of writing genres: short stories, poems, essays, informational writing, instructions for performing a task, directions, etc.

You can do this same activity for capitalization uses.

# LANGUAGE ARTS MECHANICS

**Punctuation/Independent Practice/Grades 4–8**

# Missing Punctuation

**Directions:** Choose the punctuation mark that would make the sentence correct. If no other punctuation is needed, choose "None."

**example:**  "Are you thirsty" Mother asked my sister.
         A ,     B !     C ?     D None

Read the whole sentence. Sometimes the missing punctuation can be "heard" in your mind. In this case, the ? is missing after the word *thirsty*. Mother asked sister a question. Choice C is correct.

**1.** At 7:30 every weekday, my alarm goes off.
    A ,     B !     C .     D None

**2.** "Do you enjoy baseball as much as I do?  asked Nathan.
    F !     G "     H .     J None

**3.** "Watch for the ball" shouted the coach.
    A .     B ;     C !     D None

**4.** The president of the club is J Henry.
    F ;     G ,     H .     J None

**5.** At 245 every afternoon, my bus drives up.
    A :     B !     C ,     D None

**6.** Squash potatoes, and lettuce fell to the floor when the bag broke.
    F :     G "     H ,     J None

**7.** "Do you understand the rules?" asked the game show host
    A "     B .     C :     D None

**8.** Do you have enough money for the dance
    F "     G ?     H ,     J None

**9.** Marshall likes to surf in the ocean but Jennifer would rather just walk on the shore.
    A .     B ,     C :     D None

**10.** Where are you going to put all of the old wood you found?
    F ,     G !     H "     J None

## LANGUAGE ARTS MECHANICS

**Student
Page**

Punctuation/Independent Practice/Grades 4–8

# Replacing Phrases

**Directions:** Choose the correct punctuation for the underlined part of each sentence. If no other punctuation is needed, choose "correct as it is."

**1.** Ann will decorate the tables for the <u>party and, Billy</u> will make the sandwiches.

    A    party: and Billy
    B    Party? and Billy
    C    party and, Billy
    D    party, and Billy
    E    correct as it is

**2.** <u>"It's time to leave," said</u> the guard at the auditorium door.

    F    It's time to leave, said
    G    "It's time to leave." said
    H    "It's time to leave" said
    J    It's time to leave: said
    K    correct as it is

**3.** <u>Mrs. Hendrick, our favorite coach will</u> go on the field trip with us.

    A    Mrs. Hendrick our favorite coach will
    B    Mrs. Hendrick, our favorite coach, will
    C    Mrs. Hendrick our favorite coach, will
    D    Mrs. Hendrick, our favorite coach will,
    E    correct as it is

**4.** "We need the book and a <u>pen, said</u> Mike, "if we're going to answer the questions."

    F    pen, "said
    G    pen," said
    H    pen! said
    J    pen" said
    K    correct as it is

**5.** The mixture needs <u>to set, so put</u> it in the freezer for a few hours.

    A    to set so, put
    B    to set so put,
    C    to set!  so, put
    D    to set, so put,
    E    correct as it is

# Replacing Phrases (Cont.)

**Student Page**

**6.** "Which state grows the most wheat, Kansas or <u>Nebraska" Sam</u> asked.

    F    Nebraska?" Sam
    G    Nebraska," Sam
    H    Nebraska." Sam
    J    Nebraska? Sam
    K    correct as it is

**7.** It was <u>Mrs. Jones the club sponsor</u>, who said we did a good job.

    A    Mrs. Jones, the club sponsor
    B    Mrs. Jones: the club sponsor
    C    Mrs. Jones, the club sponsor,
    D    Mrs. Jones: the club sponsor!
    E    correct as it is

**8.** These are the colors we plan to use on the <u>wall blue</u>, orange, and purple.

    F    wall, blue
    G    wall: blue,
    H    wall, blue
    J    wall, "blue
    K    correct as it is

Punctuation/Independent Practice/Grades 4–8

# Identifying Mistakes

Student
Page

**Directions:** Choose the line with a punctuation error. Choose "No mistakes" if there are no errors.

1. A  Some visitors to the museum
   B  are surprised to find statues,
   C  plaques trophies and awards.
   D  No mistakes

2. E  Travis asked to borrow my
   F  camera. I loaned it to him
   G  even though it made me nervous.
   H  No mistakes

3. A  She wrote six letters' to her
   B  friends while she was on vacation.
   C  She received only two replies.
   D  No mistakes

4. E  Jesse and his friend
   F  wanted to go to the game.  Jesses
   G  mom drove them to the field.
   H  No mistakes

5. A  My sister, who lives in Maine,
   B  collects rocks from around
   C  the world. Her collection is interesting.
   D  No mistakes

6. E  My friends always have a
   F  wonderful time, when Grandma
   G  Lisa comes to stay with us.
   H  No mistakes

7. A  "Welcome to my new home,"
   B  said Jim. "Are you hungry? We
   C  have chips, cookies, and diet, soda."
   D  No mistakes

**Punctuation/Independent Practice/Grades 4–8**

# Identifying Mistakes (Cont.)

8. E    Justin asked, "What do
   F    you get when you
   G    multiply 26 by 19
   H    No mistakes

9. A    When Jenny came home from shopping,
   B    she asked her mother and father to see
   C    "if anyone had called for her"
   D    No mistakes

10. E    Last night Ben and Jerry got
    F    lots of compliments on their
    G    ice cream. We will have them over again.
    H    No mistakes

11. A    My favorite times of the day are
    B    lunch, and dinner. Do you
    C    enjoy eating too?
    D    No mistakes

12. E    Millie can you drive to the store
    F    with me today? There isn't much
    G    time to waste.
    H    No mistakes

Punctuation/Independent Practice/Grades 4–8

# Filling in the Blanks

**Student Page**

**Directions:** Choose the word or group of words with the correct punctuation.

**1.** The five _____ test papers were lost.

    A   student's
    B   students'
    C   students
    D   students'es

**2.** To find the _____ we have to understand the map.

    E   treasure
    F   treasure;
    G   treasure:
    H   treasure,

**3.** Ada wanted to _____ all the dresses she tried on.

    A   buy and wear
    B   buy, and wear
    C   buy, and, wear
    D   buy and, wear

**4.** What is the correct way to begin a friendly letter?

    E   Dear Millie,
    F   Dear Millie
    G   Dear Millie.
    H   Dear Millie;

**5.** _____ he said he would call later.

    A   Well
    B   Well:
    C   Well,
    D   "Well"

**6.** She was _____ we were going to the concert.

    E   excited.
    F   excited
    G   excited,
    H   excited;

Punctuation/Independent Practice/Grades 4–8

# Filling in the Blanks (Cont.)

Student
Page

**7.** What is the correct way to end a letter?
     A  Sincerely,
     B  Sincerely.
     C  Sincerely
     D  Sincerely;

**8.** The doctor hesitated and _____
     E  said, "Maybe tomorrow."
     F  said "Maybe tomorrow."
     G  said, Maybe tomorrow.
     H  said Maybe tomorrow.

**9.** I saw _____ at the movie.
     A  Ms. Davis my teacher
     B  Ms. Davis, my teacher
     C  Ms. Davis my teacher,
     D  Ms. Davis, my teacher,

**10.** "Yes," said Jose, _____
     E  it was a great experience!
     F  it was a great experience!"
     G  "It was a great experience!"
     H  "it was a great experience!

# TerraNova and MAT

**TerraNova** and the **Metropolitan Achievement Test (MAT)** test language mechanics within the context of a reading passage. This sample tests for correct usage of punctuation and capitalization.

Students *must* read the sentence or phrase *in context* before deciding which answer choice, if any, makes it more correct. Sometimes there are subtle differences among the choices. Students need to understand that reading the sentence several times will help clarify for them where errors may be. Generally, more than one of the choices seems to be correct until the whole sentence is considered.

There's no substitute for practice when it comes to editing to catch errors, and no better way to approach this practice than as a group, so students can benefit from each other's ideas. Go through the following sample, item by item, taking time to thoroughly discuss each. Ideally, photocopy it onto an overhead transparency and put it on the overhead projector—it makes it much easier for everyone to see.

Autumn is my <u>favorite Season I look forward</u> to it every year. <u>There's just</u>
      **(1)**               **(2)**            **(3)**

<u>something</u> special about <u>the cool Autumn wind</u> that blows <u>around sunset it feels</u>
                                               **(4)**

<u>refreshing as it</u> clears the trees of drying leaves. Before they fall off the tree they are
        **(5)**

beautiful <u>shades of red brown yellow, and orange</u>. I enjoy putting on sweaters and

smelling smoke from fireplaces as I take my evening walk. Do you know what
                                          **(6)**

<u>my favorite Holiday is</u>. You guessed it! <u>Its Thanksgiving</u>
     **(7)**               **(8)**

1. In sentence 6, <u>my favorite Holiday is</u>. is best written:
   - A   my favorite Holiday is?
   - B   my favorite holiday is?
   - C   my favorite holiday is
   - D   As it is written

2. In sentence 8, <u>Its Thanksgiving</u> is best written:
   - E   It's Thanksgiving!
   - F   it's Thanksgiving!
   - G   it's Thanksgiving.
   - H   As it is written

3. In sentence 1, <u>favorite Season I look forward</u> is best written:

    A    favorite Season! I look forward

    B    Favorite season. I look forward

    C    favorite season. I look forward

    D    As it is written

4. In sentence 3, <u>the cool Autumn wind</u> is best written:

    E    the cool autumn wind

    F    the cool Autumn wind

    G    , the cool autumn wind

    H    As it is written

5. In sentence 4, <u>around sunset it feels refreshing as it</u> is best written:

    A    around Sunset it feels refreshing as it

    B    around sunset. It feels refreshing as it

    C    around Sunset it feels refreshing! As it

    D    As it is written

6. In sentence 5, <u>shades of red brown yellow, and orange.</u> is best written:

    E    shades of Red, Brown, Yellow, and Orange.

    F    shades of red brown, yellow, and orange.

    G    shades of red, brown, yellow, and orange.

    H    As it is written

LANGUAGE ARTS MECHANICS

**Punctuation/Independent Practice 1/Grades 4–8**

# TerraNova/MAT

Student
Page

**Directions:** Read through the rough draft. Answer the questions that follow.

Something that signals summer at our house <u>is Dad getting the charcoal</u> grill
**1**
out of the storage closet. He cleans it up with a special cleanser <u>called grill clean</u>.
**2**
Mom starts to plan which foods she will buy to cook on the <u>grill fish chicken</u>
**3**
<u>mushrooms</u>, corn, and onions. It all sounds so good to me.
**4**
When <u>im riding my yamaha moped</u> in the neighborhood with Noah and Kyle we
**5**
often smell food <u>on the grill we race</u> to our houses to see if the wonderful smell is
coming from our backyards. If <u>Kyles family is grilling he</u> often asks me to join them for
**6**
dinner. I often do the same for Kyle <u>and Carter, his brother</u>. I guess my favorite
**7**                                                                                     **8**
holiday for grilling is July 4. <u>Its such a</u> great holiday.
**9**


**1.** In sentence 1, <u>is Dad getting the charcoal</u> is best written
       A  is, Dad getting the charcoal
       B  is dad getting the charcoal
       C  is Dad getting:  the charcoal
       D  As it is written

**2.** In sentence 2, <u>called grill clean</u> is best written
       E  called, Grill Clean
       F  called:  grill clean
       G  called Grill Clean
       H  As it is written

**3.** Which sentence needs to be divided into two sentences?
       A  5
       B  4
       C  3
       D  6

**Punctuation/Independent Practice 1/Grades 4–8**

# TerraNova/MAT (Cont.)

**Student Page**

**4.** In sentence 3, <u>grill fish chicken mushrooms</u> is best written

     E  grill: fish, chicken, mushrooms,

     F  grill fish, chicken, mushrooms,

     G  grill, fish chicken mushrooms

     H  As it is written

**5.** In sentence 9, <u>Its such a</u> is best written

     A  Its such, a

     B  It's such a

     C  Its' such a

     D  As it is written

**6.** In sentence 5, <u>im riding my yamaha moped</u> is best written

     E  I'm riding my Yamaha moped

     F  I'm riding my yamaha moped

     G  i'm riding my Yamaha Moped

     H  As it is written

**7.** In sentence 5, <u>on the grill we race</u> is best written

     A  on the grill, we race

     B  on the grill. We race

     C  on the Grill. We race

     D  As it is written

**8.** In sentence 6, <u>Kyles family is grilling he</u> is best written

     E  Kyles family is grilling, he

     F  Kyles Family is grilling he

     G  Kyle's family is grilling, he

     H  As it is written

**9.** In sentence 7, and <u>Carter, his brother</u> is best written

     A  , and Carter his brother.

     B  and Carter, his Brother.

     C  and Carter his brother.

     D  As it is written

**Punctuation/Independent Practice 2/Grades 4–8**

# TerraNova/MAT

**Directions:** Read through the rough draft. Answer the questions that follow.

<u>In King Arthurs Time</u> you <u>couldn't just go</u> to the <u>fridge sink or the bathroom</u> for
1

water. You had to go to a stream or a well. And you couldn't watch <u>cable t.v.</u>! Boy,
2                                                                    3                                    4

what torture! The only book to read <u>was the bible</u>. They didn't have printers back
5                                                              6

then either. <u>A nun or a monk</u> might spend forty years copying the bible.
7

Back then some people were accused of <u>being, witches</u>. If you were accused, the
8                                                                            9

people would give you the water test. They would throw you in the water if you
10

drowned you were innocent. If you stayed afloat, you were <u>burned at the stake</u>.

Only a witch could float.
11


**1.** In sentence 1, <u>In King Arthurs Time</u> is best written:
   A   In king Arthurs Time
   B   In King Arthurs time
   C   In King Arthur's time
   D   as it is written

**2.** In sentence 1, <u>couldn't just go</u> is best written:
   A   could'nt just go
   B   couldnt' just go
   C   couldnt just, go
   D   as it is written

**3.** In sentence 1, <u>fridge sink or the bathroom</u> is best written:
   A   fridge sink, or the bathroom
   B   fridge, sink or the bathroom
   C   fridge, sink, or the bathroom
   D   as it is written

# TerraNova/MAT (Cont.)

**Student Page**

**4.** In sentence 3, <u>cable t.v.</u> is best written:
    A  cable tv
    B  cable T.V.
    C  cable TV
    D  as it is written

**5.** In sentence 5, <u>was the bible</u> is best written:
    A  was The Bible
    B  Was the bible
    C  was the Bible
    D  as it is written

**6.** In sentence 7, <u>A nun or a monk</u> is best written:
    A  a nun or a monk
    B  A Nun or a Monk
    C  A nun, or a monk
    D  as it is written

**7.** In sentence 8, <u>being, witches</u> is best written:
    A  being Witches
    B  being, Witches
    C  being witches
    D  as it is written

**8.** Which sentence needs to be divided into two sentences?
    A  8
    B  9
    C  10
    D  11

**9.** In sentence 11, <u>burned at the stake</u> is best written:
    A  burned at, the stake
    B  burned at the steak
    C  burned, at, the stake
    D  as it is written

Capitalization and Punctuation

# Test-Taking Tips

**Student Page**

@ **Take a general look** at what you are reading.  Often capitalization errors are obvious at a glance.

@ **Check for capitalization rules** that have been broken. Remember rules for proper nouns, titles, sentence beginnings, proper adjectives, certain places, etc.

@ If you are asked to choose the correct phrase, **compare the phrases word-for-word**. Don't be fooled by phrases that look almost the same.

## Punctuation

@ **Look for places where punctuation is obviously missing.** For instance, a sentence without an ending punctuation mark, or a sentence with only one set of quotation marks, needs to be fixed.

@ As you read a sentence silently, **every time you feel the need to pause** because of what the sentence is saying, you should consider putting a punctuation mark.

@ **Look for too many punctuation marks.** If a sentence looks cluttered, chances are that it may be over punctuated.

@ Think about the punctuation rules you've learned.  As you write in school and at home, **get in the habit of reviewing rules** for using commas, periods, apostrophes, quotation marks, colons and semicolons, and so on.

@ **Be aware of numbers.** There are special rules for putting punctuation marks around numbers.

# CHAPTER 5

# Language Arts Expression

As with Language Arts Mechanics, the formats used to test Language Arts Expression knowledge and skills vary from test to test and edition to edition. The list of specific topics tested within Language Arts Expression will also vary. The skills may include, but are not limited to:

- identifying correctly formed sentences
- identifying redundant sentences
- combining sentences
- choosing the correct sentence for a paragraph
- identifying simple subject and predicate
- recognizing double negatives
- identifying correct forms of verbs, adverbs, adjectives, and pronouns
- identifying sentences that do not fit
- recognizing run-on sentences
- sequencing sentences

**CAT**, **CTBS**, **ITBS**, and **SAT** test these knowledge/skill areas with individual items. A sampling of several of these formats is given. TerraNova and MAT test the knowledge/skill areas through reading passages in the same manner as with Language Arts Mechanics.

To practice spelling and reading comprehension, it is necessary for practice exercises to contain grade-level-specific vocabulary and comprehension skills. However, practicing mechanics and expression skills is possible even if the vocabulary and sentence structures used are not written specifically for a grade level. In other words, both fourth graders and eighth graders can practice capitalization, punctuation, verb tense, proper pronouns, topic sentence identification, etc., using material written for students in grades 4, 5, 6, 7 or 8. The knowledge and skills tested are not dependent on the level of difficulty of the context. For this reason, the student practice pages in this chapter are labeled "Student Practice for Grades 4-8."

Students have been exposed to so many rules when it comes to grammar. When we concentrate on one particular area in several lessons in a row, they almost get to the "automatic" stage of selecting correct answers. The trick is to help them recognize grammatical mistakes that pertain to a variety of areas all mixed together. This leads to the development of valuable editing skills.

How can we help students become discerning readers and editors? Practice is probably the best way. We want them to go about identifying mistakes, choosing correct usage, and substituting phrases in efficient ways.

## Introductory Lesson

The samples that follow require a variety of skills and formats that students may encounter on standardized tests. Photocopy pages 88–89 onto transparencies and put them on the overhead. For each item, think aloud your process toward a solution. I've provided a think-aloud comment for the first item to get you started. Once kids catch on, invite them to come up to the overhead and lead the think-aloud.

### Sample Items:

**Directions:** Choose the word or words that best completes each sentence.

1. Jonathan and _____ decided to stay at home last Friday night.
    (A)  myself
    (B)  us
    (C)  I
    (D)  me

### ⊘ Think-Aloud

"Okay, I'm going to try omitting the other subject to see which answer sounds right. If I omit *Jonathan and*, which answer choice would be correct? *Myself decided to stay...* sure doesn't sound right. *Us decided...* would make my English teacher faint. *I decided to stay...* well, that sounds right!"

*Teaching point:* Mistakes in this area are so prevalent that some of our ears may have become accustomed to *Jonathan and me*. It is important to insist on correct usage in conversation as well as in writing.

2. Can the frog jump any _____?
    (E)  highly
    (F)  highest
    (G)  more highly
    (H)  higher

*Teaching point:* Students need to hear correct usage and see it written. Point out forms of adverbs during reading and writing in all subject areas.

**Directions:** Choose the line in each item that contains a mistake. If there are no mistakes, choose "no mistakes."

3.     (A)  Even though we looked
       (B)  for two hours, we were not able

(C)  to find Williams wallet.
(D)  no mistakes

4.      (A)  For many year's we
(B)  thought the sound coming
(C)  from the garage was a squirrel.
(D)  no mistakes

*Teaching point:* From the time students are introduced to possessives and the use of the apostrophe, many of them will use an apostrophe any time an "s" is added to a word. When students revise, proof, and edit their work, arm them with an editing checklist that shows correct—and incorrect—apostrophe usage. Without explicit attention to this, students will form hard-to-break habits such as putting apostrophes on plurals.

**Directions:** Choose a word or group of words that best replaces the underlined word or group of words. If no replacement is needed, choose "no change."

5. When the teacher <u>is</u> gone, her intern took over the math lesson.
(1)  had been
(2)  was
(3)  will have been
(4)  no change

6. The two girls <u>will shop</u> all day yesterday at the mall.
(1)  will be shopping
(2)  are shopping
(3)  shopped
(4)  no change

*Teaching point:* Matching verb tense is another example of a skill that increases with awareness and practice. While many students will not write incorrectly, they will often make errors in conversation. Point out misuse when you hear it and prompt students to make their own corrections.

7. Find the simple subject.

At the end of the <u>day</u>, <u>we</u> could <u>feel</u> a sense of <u>relief</u> that our exams were over.
             A   B      C        D

8. Find the simple predicate.

We <u>were</u> much too <u>excited</u> to <u>settle</u> in for the <u>night</u>.
    A          B     C       D

*Teaching point:* Many standardized tests require students to identify parts of speech, most notably subject and predicate.  This can be practiced and reinforced every day simply by asking students to identify them regularly during any kind of reading or speaking exercise, or in conversation.

# Introductory Lesson

**Sample items:**

1. Jonathan and _____ decided to stay at home last Friday night.
   - (A)  myself
   - (B)  us
   - (C)  I
   - (D)  me

2. Can the soprano sing any _____ ?
   - (E)  highly
   - (F)  highest
   - (G)  more highly
   - (H)  higher

**Directions:** Choose the line in each item that contains a mistake. If there are no mistakes, choose "no mistakes."

3.
   - (A)  Even though we looked
   - (B)  for two hours, we were not able
   - (C)  to find Williams wallet.
   - (D)  no mistakes

4.
   - (A)  For many year's we
   - (B)  thought the sound coming
   - (C  from the garage was a squirrel.
   - (D)  no mistakes

**Directions:** Choose a word or group of words that best replaces the underlined word or group of words. If no replacement is needed, choose "no change."

5. When the teacher <u>is</u> gone, her intern took over the math lesson.
   - (1)  had been
   - (2)  was
   - (3)  will have been
   - (4)  no change

# Introductory Lesson (Cont.)

**6.** The two girls <u>will shop</u> all day yesterday at the mall.
- (1)   will be shopping
- (2)   are shopping
- (3)   shopped
- (4)   no change

**7.** Find the simple subject.

At the end of the <u>day</u>, <u>we</u> could <u>feel</u> a sense of <u>relief</u> that our exams were over.
              A     B          C             D

**8.** Find the simple predicate.

We <u>were</u> much too <u>excited</u> to <u>settle</u> in for the <u>night</u>.
  A              B        C         D

**Punctuation/Independent Practice/Grades 4–8**

# Filling in the Blank

Student
Page

**Directions:** Choose the word or words that best completes each sentence.

Can that frog jump any _____?
- A highly
- B higher
- C highest
- D more highly

It is important to read the sentence with each of the words or phrases filling in the blank. Think about how they sound.

- A Can that frog jump any <u>highly</u>?
- B Can that frog jump any <u>higher</u>?
- C Can that frog jump any <u>highest</u>?
- D Can that frog jump any <u>more highly</u>?

Choice B is correct.

---

I _____ my new album to work Monday.
- E will bring
- F have brought
- G brings
- H bring

- E <u>I will bring</u> my new album to work next Monday.
- F <u>I have brought</u> my new album to work next Monday.
- G <u>I brings</u> my new album to work next Monday.
- H <u>I bring</u> my new album to work next Monday.

Choice E gives us the future tense we need to do something next Monday.

---

**1.** Janet made a salad for _____ lunch.
- A me
- B my
- C mine
- D myself

**2.** The president wrote a memo to _____.
- E yourself
- F him
- G he
- H his

# LANGUAGE ARTS EXPRESSION

**Punctuation/Independent Practice/Grades 4–8**

# Filling in the Blank (Cont.)

**Student Page**

**3.** Jerry _____ the table for our party.

    A    sets

    B    am setting

    C    is setting

    D    are setting

**4.** The giraffe is _____ than the elephant.

    E    tall

    F    taller

    G    tallest

    H    more tall

**5.** He spoke _____ to the young group.

    A    clear

    B    clearly

    C    clearing

    D    more clearer

**6.** That is the _____ dress at the party tonight.

    E    unique

    F    uniquest

    G    more unique

    H    most unique

**7.** _____ are working at the theatre Tuesday.

    A    He and I

    B    Him and me

    C    He and me

    D    Him and I

**8.** Aunt Sara _____ you to the play tomorrow night.

    E    will drive

    F    drive

    G    drove

    H    had driven

LANGUAGE ARTS EXPRESSION

**Independent Practice/Grades 4–8**

# Identifying Mistakes

**Directions:** Choose the line in each item that contains a mistake. If there are no mistakes, choose "no mistakes."

**Ex. 1.**
A  My best friend wants to know
B  how to play the game Monopoly
C  so I'm learning him to play it.
D  no mistakes

Always read the item before looking for mistakes. Sometimes they leap out as you read! In this item *learning* is the wrong verb, so mark C.

**Ex. 2.**
E  When we got to the store, Dad
F  said, "Let's all meet back here
G  at the entrance in one hour."
H  no mistakes

This sounds good the first time through. Read it again slowly. Does it still sound correct? If so, mark "no mistakes."

**Ex. 3.**
A  My aunt and uncle goes to the
B  movies every week. They always
C  eat so much popcorn!
D  no mistakes

Here we have a problem with subject-verb agreement in line A. The subject is plural, meaning there are two people. The verb *goes* should only be used with a singular subject.

1.  E  It is so much fun to watch the
    F  kitten try to wash hisself. he
    G  just rolls all over the floor.
    H  no mistakes

2.  A  The jazz concert was very
    B  entertaining. We were all
    C  pleased at how well Mike singed.
    D  no mistakes

3.  E  I should ought to have done
    F  my homework earlier. Now I'm too
    G  tired to even think about it!
    H  no mistakes

# LANGUAGE ARTS EXPRESSION

**Independent Practice/Grades 4–8**

# Identifying Mistakes (Cont.)

**Student Page**

4.  A    Mom wondered to
    B    who Ann was speaking when
    C    she yelled, "Leave it alone!"
    D    no mistakes

5.  E    Haven't you never been to
    F    Aunt Edith's house? She lives
    G    right around the corner from me.
    H    no mistakes

6.  A    My favoritist actress Helen
    B    Hunt. She was really good in
    C    the movie *Twister*.
    D    no mistakes

7.  E    My sister and me cooked hamburgers
    F    last night, and everyone, even
    G    my dad, said they were delicious.
    H    no mistakes

8.  A    Jamal and Marvin saved their money
    B    and bought their selves a CD player.
    C    Music makes them feel happy.
    D    no mistakes

9.  E    The game was exciting, and I maked three
    F    baskets. Next time I'll try to make
    G    four or more.
    H    no mistakes

10. A    The next time us come here
    B    we will try to see Jesse.
    C    He has been working lately.
    D    no mistakes

Independent Practice/Grades 4–8

# Word and Phrase Replacement

**Directions:** Choose the word or group of words that best replaces the underlined word or group of words. If no replacement is needed, choose "no change."

April enjoys her job <u>finding and buying</u> birthday gifts for clients.
- A  finding, buying
- B  to find and to buy
- C  being the finding and buying of
- D  no change

It is important to take time to read the sentence four times, first as it is and then with A, B, and C replacing what is underlined. Concentrate on what your mind hears as you read silently.

April enjoys her job finding and buying birthday gifts for clients.
April enjoys her job finding, buying birthday gifts for clients.
April enjoys her job to find and to buy birthday gifts for clients.
April enjoys her job being the finding and buying of birthday gifts for clients.

Which "sounds" best in your mind? If you chose the first sentence, you are correct. It does not need to be changed, so the answer is D.

........................................................................................................................

**1.** No matter how well the Jets play, I'll be their fan <u>that</u> I live in New York.
- E  but
- F  as long as
- G  during
- H  no change

**2.** It's easier for me to do my chores <u>be until</u> it is daylight.
- A  when
- B  so that
- C  unless
- D  no change

**3.** The dentist always reminds us to brush and floss our teeth <u>while</u> bedtime.
- E  until
- F  before
- G  since
- H  no change

Independent Practice/Grades 4–8

# Word and Phrase Replacement (Cont.)

**Student
Page**

**4.** When we see each other in October, summer <u>was</u> over.
     A  had been
     B  is being
     C  will be
     D  no change

**5.** Now that it is autumn, we <u>did get</u> plenty of chilly weather.
     E  will be getting
     F  had been getting
     G  got
     H  no change

**6.** <u>Except</u> you lose your confidence, you'll do well on the program.
     A  Unless
     B  Besides
     C  Since
     D  no change

**7.** Tyrone <u>won</u> a jogging competition last month.
     E  will win
     F  winning
     G  wins
     H  no change

**8.** My friend sent his girlfriend a dozen roses <u>if</u> he loves her.
     A  because
     B  until
     C  then
     D  no change

**9.** James Taylor <u>be</u> one of my favorite singers.
     E  is
     F  should be
     G  are
     H  no change

Independent Practice/Grades 4–8

# Subject and Predicate

**Directions:** Find the simple subject of each sentence.

The <u>lovely</u> <u>bird</u> <u>came</u> quietly to the <u>feeder</u>.
    A    B    C               D

There are four choices for the simple subject. The first thing you need to do is think back to what a subject is. *Lovely* describes the bird, *came* tells what the bird did and *feeder* tells where the action took place. So the subject is *bird*.

**1.** Large <u>dogs</u> <u>need</u> a lot of <u>space</u> to run and <u>play</u>.
       E    F       G         H

**2.** The <u>hanging</u> <u>ladder</u> <u>was</u> a part of the <u>scheme</u> to escape.
     A     B   C          D

**3.** <u>Blue</u> and <u>green</u> <u>paper</u> covered the <u>shelves</u>.
  E       F  G        H

**4.** <u>Many</u> <u>large</u> <u>containers</u> lined the <u>wall</u>.
  A    B   C        D

**Directions:** Find the simple predicate of each sentence.

In the <u>middle</u> of the <u>night</u> I <u>heard</u> her <u>scream</u>.
      E        F  G     H

There are four choices for the predicate. Remember that the predicate is the verb— the action of the phrase or sentence. *Middle* and *night* both tell when the action occurred. *Scream* tells what was *heard*. So the verb is *heard*.

**5.** The <u>book</u> <u>looks</u> <u>interesting</u> to <u>me</u>.
    A    B    C    D

**6.** The <u>neighborhood</u> craft <u>fair</u> <u>begins</u> <u>tomorrow</u>.
      E         F  G    H

**7.** An <u>apple</u> from the <u>southern</u> <u>orchard</u> <u>tastes</u> best.
    A         B    C    D

**8.** Too few <u>bicycle</u> <u>designs</u> <u>passed</u> the safety <u>test</u>.
       E    F   G       H

# Grammar Test-Taking Strategies

Student Page

**1** **Be very aware of how a sentence sounds.** It is usually possible to identify incorrect use of word forms simply by paying attention to how words sound together. Read and reread silently to yourself and trust your instincts when words and phrases sound "off."

**2** **Remember rules** for identifying subjects, objects, verbs, adjectives, adverbs, and so on.

**3** **To identify complete sentences**, look for groups of words that have both a subject and a verb.

**4** **Be sure groups of words express a complete thought before you call them a sentence.** For instance, "Tony's story, rained all day" has a possible subject—*story*—and a possible verb—*rained*—but the story didn't rain!

**5** **Watch for run-on sentences!** If a sentence contains two complete thoughts without a connecting word, chances are that it is a run-on sentence. It would be better written as two sentences.

**6** **When combining sentences**, make sure the meaning of the new sentence is the same as the meanings of the two original sentences.

**7** **Be careful to use the right conjunction** when combining thoughts. Using words such as *and, but, since, therefore,* etc., in the wrong way can change the whole meaning of a sentence.

**8** **When sequencing sentences**, look for words such as *then, next, first, before,* etc., to help in finding the order of events.

**9** **To find a sentence that does not belong**, look for ideas that do not relate to the main idea of the paragraph. They could be perfectly fine sentences with valuable information, but not information that fits the rest of the paragraph.

# Combining Sentences

Combining sentences can be tricky for students. There are very few rules. To combine sentences requires judgment and being able to hear what sounds right. This is tough to teach and hard to learn for middle-level kids. They need lots of practice. On tests, sometimes all four choices are technically correct, but one is considered best. Nevertheless, there are some guidelines that will help students. Put the following tips on a posterboard so kids can refer to them often.

---

### Guidelines for Combining Sentences

1. All active verbs should be repeated.
2. Identical adjectives/adverbs, and adjective/adverb phrases, should not be repeated.
3. Different adjectives should be used in front of the subject with the word *and*.
4. Direct objects should not be repeated.
5. No additional meaning may be added to the original sentences.
6. All significant information should be included.

---

## Introductory Lesson

Say to students, "Combining sentences is something we do every day and we don't even think about it... Hey, I just did it!"

Write on blackboard: Combining sentences is something we do every day. We don't even think about it.

"I had these two complete thoughts and combined them when I spoke to you... I did it again!"

Write on board:  I had these two complete thoughts.
I combined them when I spoke to you.

Refer to first two sentences: "All I did here was put *and* between the two sentences."
Refer to second two sentences: "It makes sense to me to use *and*, leaving out the second *I*.
In conversation and in writing we naturally combine complete thoughts or sentences to 'sound right.'"

Refer to poster: "There are few hard and fast rules for combining sentences. What we have are guidelines. I'm going to think aloud through some examples."
(Put examples from page 99 on transparencies to show while thinking aloud.)

# LANGUAGE ARTS EXPRESSION

**Example 1**

Directions: Read both sentences. Choose the best way to combine them into one sentence.

1. The student brought the tickets to school.
   The student gave a ticket to each classmate.

   A  The student gave tickets to his classmates.
   B  The student brought the tickets to school and gave one to each classmate.
   C  The student brought the tickets to school and gave a ticket to each classmate.
   D  The student brought the tickets to school because his classmates wanted them.

### ◎ Think-Aloud

"Let's see... I've got two main thoughts here. I know the tickets were brought to school and then were given to classmates. Choice A doesn't say anything about school. That's significant. Guideline 6 says all information should be included. Choice B looks good—all the information is there and it sounds right when I read it to myself. Choice C sounds okay, but guideline 4 says I shouldn't repeat direct objects like *ticket*. Choice B referred to *ticket* as *one*. I think that's better than Choice C. Choice D really adds something. It says the tickets were brought to school because they were wanted. That may be true, but the original sentences don't say it... Hmmm, Choice B looks best to me."

That's a lot of explanation for one item, but we can see that it helps clarify the guidelines. Do another with students. Here are some ideas to use when thinking aloud using Example 2.

**Example 2**

2. John bought a tent for the camping trip.
   The tent was brown.
   The tent was expensive.

   A  The tent was brown and expensive and John bought it.
   B  John had enough money to buy an expensive tent for the camping trip.
   C  The tent that John bought for the camping trip was brown and expensive.
   D  John bought an expensive brown tent for the camping trip.

### ◎ Think-Aloud

Choice D is correct. Choice A needlessly repeats *and*. Choice B changes the meaning of the original sentences. Choice C is the one many students might choose because it reads nicely and conveys the message completely. However, when compared to Choice D, it is more cumbersome and contains an unnecessary *and*.

Do as many think-alouds as a class as you feel students need, using examples from the Independent Practice pages or ones of your own making. Have students work with partners to tackle items together.

Independent Practice/Grades 4–8

# Combining Sentences

**Student Page**

**1.** The Sahara is the largest desert in the world.
It stretches across all of North Africa.

A  The Sahara stretches across all of North Africa because it is the largest desert in the world.
B  The largest desert in the world the Sahara stretches across all of North Africa.
C  The largest desert in the world stretches across all of North Africa, the Sahara.
D  Stretching across all of North Africa is the largest desert in the world, the Sahara.

**2.** The Sahara contains about 90 large oases.
An oasis is a place with water.

A  The Sahara has about 90 large oases, with water.
B  The Sahara contains about 90 large oases, and an oasis is a place with water.
C  There are about 90 large oases of water in the Sahara.
D  The Sahara has about 90 large places with water, oases.

**3.** Each oasis is fed from an underground spring.
The water allows trees, other plants, animals, and people to live there.

A  Trees, plants, animals, and people live at each oasis.
B  An underground spring feeds each oasis with water and plants, trees, people, and animals live there.
C  Each oasis has water which allows plants, animals, trees, and people to live at each oasis.
D  Water from the underground spring that feeds each oasis allows trees, other plants, animals, and people to live there.

**4.** Mexico is our neighbor to the south.
It has long, hot summers and warm winters.

A  Mexico, our neighbor to the south, has long, hot summers and warm winters.
B  Summers in Mexico, our neighbor to the south, are long and hot, but winters are warm there.
C  Our neighbor to the south, Mexico, has long, hot summers, and mild winters.
D  Summers are long and hot, and winters are mild, in our neighbor to the south, Mexico.

Independent Practice/Grades 4–8

# Combining Sentences (Cont.)

Student Page

**5.** My friend Angela was sick today.
We did not go to the movies.

A Today my friend Angela was sick, and we did not go to the movies.
B My friend Angela was sick today so we did not go the the movies.
C Angela, my friend, today was sick because we did not go to the movies.
D My friend Angela was sick, and today we did not go to the movies.

**6.** Each fall we pick apples for cider.
My father presses the juice out.

A Each fall my father presses the juice out and we pick apples for cider.
B For cider we pick apples each fall, but my father presses the juice out.
C We pick apples for cider each fall, and my father presses the juice out.
D Each fall my father presses the juice out for cider, after we pick the apples.

**7.** Dolphins are air-breathing fish.
They hold their breath under water like you and me.

A Dolphins are air-breathing fish that hold their breath like you and me when they swim under water.
B Dolphins hold their breath under water because they are air-breathing fish, like you and me.
C Like you and me dolphins hold their breath under water and are air-breathing fish.
D By holding their breath under water dolphins are air-breathing fish like you and me.

**8.** Owls hunt for food at night.
Owls can see in the dark.

A Owls can see in the dark and hunt for food at night.
B Owls can hunt for food at night so they can see in the dark.
C By seeing in the dark owls hunt for food at night.
D Owls, which can see in the dark, hunt for food at night.

**9.** The bread was baking in the oven.
Samuel loved the wonderful smell.

A The wonderful smell of baking bread is what Samuel loved in the oven.
B Samuel loved the wonderful smell of bread baking in the oven.
C The bread was baking and, Samuel loved the wonderful smell in the oven.
D In the oven, Samuel loved the wonderful smell of bread baking.

LANGUAGE ARTS EXPRESSION ⌐ ■ ■ ⌐ ■ ⌐ ■ ⌐ ■ ⌐

# Choosing Topic Sentences

All of the choices given as possibilities for topic sentences are structurally fine. When read by themselves, students cannot pick out the best choice from among the options. Reading the whole paragraph is vital. Perhaps the best way to eliminate one or more choices is to look for sentences that make reference only to pronouns such as *it, they, he, she,* etc. The topic sentence should have a clearly stated subject. An effective way to practice the skill of choosing a topic sentence is to put a practice paragraph that is missing a topic sentence on the chalkboard or an overhead transparency for all of the class to read. Lead the students in a discussion of the important information. Ask each one to write a topic sentence for the paragraph and then to share their sentences in their cooperative groups. The groups then decide how to put their individual sentences together to make the best topic sentence. The groups take turns sharing their sentences. (See activity, page 103.) If students practice writing their own sentences, they are much more likely to recognize appropriate topic sentences.

**Directions:** Read each paragraph. Choose the best topic sentence.

1. _____. Some people welcome them because they tend to cool off very hot days. Drooping plants seem to come back to life when the rain drenches the soil. Thunderstorms give me a reason to rest for a while as I sit on the front porch and watch the power of nature.

A   Plants need water on very hot days.
B   Thunderstorms on a summer afternoon often bring relief.
C   They seem to come up so quickly.
D   Weather forecasters help us to know how to plan our days.

*Teaching point:* Choice B is correct. The paragraph is not about plants or weather forecasters. Choice C could be about thunderstorms, but *they* is not defined.

2. _____. If you have never been on a dairy farm or watched a video about milking cows, you may not have noticed the three legs. A stool with three legs will stay balanced even if one of the legs is shorter or if the ground is uneven. If there are four legs, and one is shorter or on an uneven surface, the stool will rock back and forth. Try it for yourself.

E   Dairy farms are big business in the United States.
F   The furniture industry has a lot to learn about making chairs.
G   It is interesting to see how cows are milked.
H   Have you ever wondered why a milking stool has three legs instead of four?

*Teaching point:* Choice H is correct. It introduces the topic of three-legged stools. The paragraph is not about dairy farms, the furniture industry, or how to milk cows.

# Choosing Topic Sentences

## Group Activity

**Great Beginnings: Add a Topic Sentence!**

This activity involves both individual work and group participation. It is an effective way to practice the skills of choosing topic sentences.

1. Put up an overhead transparency that contains a paragraph that does not have a good topic sentence.
2. Talk through the important information in the paragraph.
3. Have students each write a topic sentence they think improves the piece. Ask students to share their sentences in small groups.
4. Groups may either choose the sentence they feel is best or write a sentence putting together the best of their ideas.
5. Each group will paste their topic sentence on a posterboard containing the rest of the paragraph.
6. This activity may be repeated as many times as desired.

If students practice writing their own topic sentences, they are much more likely to recognize appropriate topic sentences when they see them.


1. _____. There are over 110 million drivers licensed in the United States, and over 15 million of them are teenagers. But as the number of cars on the road has increased, automobile accidents have also soared. Records show that most teenage accidents are caused by inexperienced drivers who make mistakes because they don't understand or obey traffic laws.

2. _____. In most states, new drivers must secure a learner's permit before qualifying for a driver's license. The permit allows them to practice driving, but only under certain conditions. For example, there must be a licensed driver in the car, and in many states the learner must practice only in designated areas, and not after dark.

3. _____. After the driver applies the brakes, a car can still travel quite a distance. A car going 40 miles an hour will travel 116 feet before it stops! A good driver can sense trouble ahead of time. So when the time comes for you to get behind the wheel, look ahead, keep your eyes open, and obey all traffic laws.

LANGUAGE ARTS EXPRESSION

**Teacher-Directed Student Practice/Grades 4–8**

# Choosing Topic Sentences

**Directions:** Read each paragraph. Choose the best topic sentence.

1. _____. Some people welcome them because they tend to cool off very hot days. Drooping plants seem to come back to life when the rain drenches the soil. Thunderstorms give me a reason to rest for a while as I sit on the front porch and watch the power of nature.

A   Plants need water on very hot days.
B   Thunderstorms on a summer afternoon often bring relief.
C   They seem to come up so quickly.
D   Weather forecasters help us to know how to plan our days.

2. _____. If you have never been on a dairy farm or watched a video about milking cows, you may not have noticed the three legs. A stool with three legs will stay balanced even if one of the legs is shorter or if the ground is uneven. If there are four legs, and one is shorter or on an uneven surface, the stool will rock back and forth. Try it for yourself.

E   Dairy farms are big business in the United States.
F   The furniture industry has a lot to learn about making chairs.
G   It is interesting to see how cows are milked.
H   Have you ever wondered why a milking stool has three legs instead of four?

Independent Practice/Grades 4–8

# Choosing Topic Sentences

Student
Page

**1.** _____. The birds are bred in captivity and then released into big cities. Peregrine falcons live in the mountains, and it is hoped that the jagged skyline will make them feel at home. The cities are also free of the great horned owl, the falcons' chief enemy. So far, the falcons seem to be adapting. They are nesting atop buildings and preying on local pigeons and sparrows.

A    Big cities provide an ideal home for some birds.
B    Not all birds get along in the wild.
C    Scientists are taking unusual steps to save the endangered peregrine falcons.
D    Buildings and birds sometimes go together.

**2.** _____. Davy Crockett was born in Tennessee in 1786. He joined the army and fought the War of 1812. After the war, Davy was elected to the state legislature and then to Congress three times.  He was a gifted storyteller and he himself was usually the hero in his own tall tales. In 1835 Crockett moved to Texas, where he lost his life defending the Alamo from the Mexican army.

A    Davy Crockett is one of the most colorful and beloved heroes of the Old West.
B    We ought to celebrate the heroes of the Western Movement.
C    People suffered many hardships as they moved west.
D    Davy Crockett was Tennessee's first famous politician.

**3.** _____. Crumple a piece of paper to make a ball and push it into a tall glass so it fits snugly against the sides and bottom of the glass. Turn the glass upside down and immerse it, mouth facing straight down, into a bowl of water. Now lift it straight up, out of the water. Wipe the edges dry before turning the glass right side up. Take out the paper. It's quite dry, isn't it?

A    Here's a great magic trick you can do to keep paper dry under water.
B    Paper doesn't always stay dry when you put it in water.
C    If you crumple paper tightly enough it will not soak up water.
D    How about those Mets?

**4.** _____. Even though we can't see air, it takes up space. When you lowered the glass into water, the air remained in the glass. The air kept the water from reaching the paper inside the glass.  Air was still in the glass as you lifted it out of the water. That's why the paper stayed dry.

A    Air is colorless, tasteless, and invisible.
B    There's a scientific explanation for this magic trick.
C    The paper traps some air in the glass.
D    Look for the air bubble in the glass.

# Using Editing to Reinforce and Test

The **Metropolitan Achievement Test** and the **TerraNova** assess Language Arts Expression through the editing process. All the skills practiced so far in this chapter are contained within the "rough draft" passages given on these two major tests. The instructions say to answer questions that refer to the rough draft given to students to analyze. If students are not familiar with this particular format, they will be thwarted by confusion. However, if we "look at the forest rather than the trees," the **Metropolitan Achievement Test** and **TerraNova** formats align more closely with real-world uses of Language Arts Expression skills.

Let's take a closer look at this direct editing format in the example that follows:

My friend and I is planning a big party for next week. Anna will buy the supplies I
1                                                                                   2

will buy the gifts for everyone. We was thinking about renting the Parker Pavillion. Too
3                                                                                   4

much money. We will be shopping all day at the mall.
5

1. Choose the best way to write sentence 1.

A    My friend and I is planning for next week a big party.
B    I and my friend is planning a big party for next week.
C    My friend and I are planning a big party for next week.
D    I and my friend are planning a big party for next week.

*Teaching point:* Subject-verb agreement problems are among the most noticeable to the listener. If students are around people who practice proper agreement, they will quickly pick up on mistakes when they hear them. There are two subjects in sentence 1: *friend* and *I*. Therefore, the verb should be plural: *are*. The correct choice is C. Remind students that in a series of names, *I* goes last.

2. Which sentence either needs to be two sentences or needs a semicolon?

E    Sentence 2
F    Sentence 3
G    Sentence 4
H    Sentence 5

*Teaching point:* Choice E is correct. There are two distinct thoughts here without a conjunction. A period between *supplies* and *I* would cure the problem. The conjunction *and* between the two words would work. A semicolon between them would also make it correct. Here are the possibilities:

Anna will buy the supplies. I will buy the gifts.
Anna will buy the supplies and I will buy the gifts.
Anna will buy the supplies; I will buy the gifts.

3. Which word needs to be changed in sentence 3 to make it grammatically correct?

A   about
B   was
C   We
D   renting

*Teaching Point:* Here's another subject-verb agreement problem. *We* is plural so the verb should also be plural. The word *was* should be *were*, so choice B is correct.

4. Which is not a proper sentence?

E   Sentence 1
F   Sentence 3
G   Sentence 4
H   Sentence 5

*Teaching point:* We must have a subject and a verb to make a sentence. *Too much money* is a phrase containing neither. Choice G is correct.

# LANGUAGE ARTS EXPRESSION

# Editing

Give students copies of the Teacher-Directed Student Practice form on pages 111–112. As a class, talk about each item. Below are comments to guide your discussion.

**Directions:** Read the rough draft carefully, then answer the questions. When your teacher says to, discuss your answers with a neighbor. Mark questions you disagree on. Your teacher will lead the whole class in a discussion.

Have you ever been camping? I can tell you that camping can be fun and
(1)                                                    (2)

exciting. It can be enjoyable. It gives you a chance to experience the outdoors. For
         (3)                    (4)                                              (5)

example, an example of this are smells, sights, and sounds in the outdoors that you

can never find in a town or a city. Yellowstone National Park has some great
                                        (6)

campsites. You can enjoy swimming, canoeing, and hiking. You can spend time and
           (7)                                            (8)

have fun with your family and friends. And your pets.
                                          (9)

Camping is also an affordable way to go on vacation. A campsite costs about
(10)                                                  (11)

$15 and just as eating at home you can have meals for about the same cost. You can
                                                                      (12)

cook these meals on an open fire or cook them on a camp stove.

**1.** What is the topic sentence of the second paragraph?

    A   12

    B   11

    C   10

    D   1

*Teaching point:* Choice C is correct. Choices A and B describe why camping is affordable. Choice D is not even in the second paragraph.

**2.** Which group of words is not a complete sentence?

    E   3

    F   9

    G   11

    H   12

*Teaching Point:* Choice F is correct. Choices E, G, and H all have subjects and predicates.

## LANGUAGE ARTS EXPRESSION

# Editing (Cont.)

**3.** Which of the following sentences best combines sentence 2 and sentence 3 without changing their meanings?

A   I can tell you a lot about camping, fun, exciting, enjoyable.
B   I can tell you that camping can be things such as fun, exciting, and enjoyable.
C   I can tell you that camping can be fun, exciting, and enjoyable.
D   Fun, exciting, and enjoyable is what I can tell you that camping is.

*Teaching point:* Choice C is correct. Choice A doesn't "sound" right; in fact, it sounds just plain incorrect! Choice B is probably second best, but has unnecessary words in it—"things such as." Choice D sounds backwards.

**4.** What is the best way to write sentence 5?

E   An example of an example are smells, sights, and sounds that you can never find in a town or a city.
F   There are smells, sights, and sounds in the outdoors that you can never find in a town or a city.
G   There are smells, sights, and sounds in the outdoors, for example, that are different than the smells, sights, and sounds in a city.
H   As it is written.

*Teaching point:* Choice F is correct. Choice E uses *example* twice. Choice G repeats "smell, sights, and sounds."

**5.** Which of the following sentences could be added before sentence 7?

A   My favorite part of camping is roasting marshmallows.
B   There are many activities you can enjoy.
C   At camping, everyone dresses comfortably.
D   My family usually goes camping four or five times a year.

*Teaching point:* Choice B is correct. Sentence 7 lists things to do while camping, so a sentence stating that there are many activities makes sense as a good addition.

**6.** What is the most colorful way to write sentence 12?

E   You can cook delicious meals on a crackling open fire or cook them on a camp stove.
F   You can cook meals on a fire or a stove.
G   You can cook some of the meals on a fire and some on a stove.
H   As it is written.

# LANGUAGE ARTS EXPRESSION

## Editing (Cont.)

*Teaching point:* Choice E is correct. Choice F and G say about the same thing, but they are boring. Unless it has been pointed out, students don't understand the meaning of *colorful* as it applies to writing. They need to practice colorful writing themselves. Teachers can give students a "bare bones" sentence and ask them to dress it up.

**7.** Which sentence contains information that does not belong in the article?

A   3
B   4
C   6
D   8

*Teaching point:* Choice C is correct. Choices A and B speak directly to the subject of camping. Choice D gives major benefits of camping. If A, B, and D weren't such strong contributors, telling about a specific camping sight would be correct.

# LANGUAGE ARTS EXPRESSION

**Teacher-Directed Student Practice/Grades 4–8**

# Editing

Student
Page

**Directions:** Read the rough draft carefully. Then answer the questions.

Have you ever been camping? I can tell you that camping can be fun and
(1)                                                  (2)

exciting. It can be enjoyable. It gives you a chance to experience the outdoors. For
(3)                (4)                                                              (5)

example, an example of this are smells, sights, and sounds in the outdoors that you

can never find in a town or a city. Yellowstone National Park has some great
(6)

campsites. You can enjoy swimming, canoeing, and hiking. You can spend time and
(7)                                                        (8)

have fun with your family and friends. And your pets.
(9)

Camping is also an affordable way to go on vacation. A campsite costs about
(10)                                                        (11)

$15 and just as eating at home you can have meals for about the same cost. You can
(12)

cook these meals on an open fire or cook them on a camp stove.

**1.** What is the topic sentence of the second paragraph?
A   12
B   11
C   10
D   1

**2.** Which group of words is not a complete sentence?
E   3
F   9
G   11
H   12

**3.** Which of the following sentences best combines sentence 2 and sentence 3 without changing their meanings?
A   I can tell you a lot about camping, fun, exciting, enjoyable.
B   I can tell you that camping can be things such as fun, exciting, and enjoyable.
C   I can tell you that camping can be fun, exciting, and enjoyable.
D   Fun, exciting, and enjoyable is what I can tell you that camping is.

Teacher Directed Student Practice/Grades 4–8

# Editing (Cont.)

**4.** What is the best way to write sentence 5?

E An example of an example are smells, sights, and sounds that you can never find in a town or a city.

F There are smells, sights, and sounds in the outdoors that you can never find in a town or a city.

G There are smells, sights, and sounds in the outdoors, for example, that are different than the smells, sights, and sounds in a city.

H As it is written.

**5.** Which of the following sentences could be added before sentence 7?

A My favorite part of camping is roasting marshmallows.

B There are many activities you can enjoy.

C At camping, everyone dresses comfortably.

D My family usually goes camping four or five times a year.

**6.** What is the most colorful way to write sentence 12?

E You can cook delicious meals on a crackling open fire or cook them on a camp stove.

F You can cook meals on a fire or a stove.

G You can cook some of the meals on a fire and some on a stove.

H As it is written.

**7.** Which sentence contains information that does not belong in the article?

A 3

B 4

C 6

D 8

# CHAPTER 6

# Spelling

"I'm a terrible speller!" is an often heard, almost socially acceptable, lament of both school-age children and adults. Vocabulary, both spelling and definitions, must be taught hand-in-hand with reading and writing instruction. Middle and high school students who find themselves lacking a firm grasp in these areas will be seriously handicapped by their inability to adequately show what they know about the content in all subjects.

## Letter Groupings

There are letter groupings that occur and recur in our language. Recognizing these groupings will trigger a student's memory and increase spelling proficiency. Of course, not only will spelling skills improve, but so will vocabulary usage. Here are some of the categories of letter groupings that students have learned about prior to the middle grades. Whether we need to reteach these categories, or simply remind students of them, depends on the proficiency level of students as well as grade level.

A **prefix** is a group of letters added to the beginning of a word. A prefix changes the meaning of a word. Each prefix changes the words it precedes in the same way. Some common prefixes include:

| | | | | |
|---|---|---|---|---|
| un- | dis- | mis- | anti- | fore- |
| in- | re- | im- | con- | super- |

A **suffix** is a group of letters or a single letter added to the end of a word. A suffix changes the meaning of a word. Each suffix changes the word it follows in the same way. Some common suffixes include:

| | | | | | |
|---|---|---|---|---|---|
| -less | -al | -ment | -able | -ture | -s |
| -ful | -sion | -ly | -ness | -ing | -es |

There are letter groupings that form rhymes. These groupings are very common, and instant recognition of them will help students connect new words with familiar words. Some of these groupings include:

| | | | | |
|---|---|---|---|---|
| ack | ed | ill | op | un |
| at | en | in | it | ub |
| an | ell | it | ock | use |

| ag | et  | ip  | old | ute |
|----|-----|-----|-----|-----|
| ap | est | ice | ow  | une |
| ay | ee  | ide | oke | urt |

It is important to equip students who are acquiring reading skills with all the spelling skills possible so they will be confident in their spelling abilities, and have an appreciation for spelling correctness. Exposure to a variety of words that are rotated on and off the classroom walls will increase familiarity and encourage students to use a wider vocabulary. Words chosen for emphasis may come from lists of frequently used words, the most misspelled words in actual classroom use, lists developed by publishers/district personnel, content-specific words, and so forth.

There are some traditional steps that may help students learn to spell a word. These steps include, but are not limited to:

- Look at the word and say the letters.
- Think about the sound of each letter and/or blend.
- Close your eyes and "picture" the word.
- With your eyes closed, practice spelling the word.
- Practice writing the word several times.
- Use the word in conversation and writing exercises.

# Spelling on Standardized Tests

There are some general guidelines for students to keep in mind when faced with a standardized spelling test. Here are a few to share with your class:

- Reading directions is crucial. Some tests ask for students to identify the word spelled incorrectly while others ask for the correct word to be identified.

- Does the word "look" right? Students need to be exposed to the power of visual learning.

- *Homophones* are words that are pronounced the same, have different meanings, and are spelled differently. They are often the most frequently misspelled words—or misidentified as misspelled words. There are numerous practice books that expose students to the large number of homophones in the English language. Having students generate all the class can think of and then do sentence writing, illustrations, flashcards, etc. with the homophones can be quite helpful in heightening awareness.

- Students should look for words, or segments of words, to which they may apply the spelling rules they have practiced since primary grades.

The spelling formats of some of the major standardized tests are given below.

**MAT 7**: sentence with three underlined words, one of which may be misspelled, plus a "no mistake" option

**SAT 9**: same as MAT 7

**CTBS**: 1. sentence with blank, four spelling options of one word to fill in the blank; 2. three phrases with all words spelled correctly, one phrase with a misspelled word

**ITBS**: four different words, three correct, possibly one misspelled, plus a "no mistake" option

## How Should We Teach Spelling?

We face the same dilemma at the beginning of every year: what words should we require students to learn to spell correctly? Of course we want them to spell every word correctly. When we edit we always look for spelling errors. This is good for students, and we will continue the process of finding, and then correcting spelling errors. It makes sense. However, there are words that need to be emphasized and then tested. The "official" list may come from the state department of education, the district, or a curriculum coordinator. The words on the list may be generated from "most frequently used" sources, adopted texts, or a specific reading program. Students need to know how to spell words on "most frequently used" lists. They need to know how to spell words that go with the units and content taught in their grade level. Students and teachers alike understand the value of knowing how to spell the words they use every day. We emphasize them. Now how do we know we're even getting close to the words the students will need to know how to spell on the standardized test next spring? Unless the publisher puts out a list, we don't know.

The best tactic is to help students discover patterns and rules of spelling. In the English language it is easy to get frustrated because so many rules are broken and so many patterns are violated. Students are old enough to understand this. Be honest with them. We'll probably learn a lot by looking at the exceptions, as well as the rules. We need a way to present patterns and rules. Let's call them *strategies*. How about "Word Attack Strategies"! Here's a brief list to begin with.

### Word Attack Strategies

When a word has double consonants, as in *better* and *ladder*, only one is sounded.

A one-syllable word ending in a vowel results in the vowel using its long sound.

In a word with a vowel and an *e* at the end, the ending *e* is silent.

If a word has the blend *kn*, the *k* is silent.

If a word begins with *ph*, the combined sound is that of *f*.

If a word begins with *wr*, the *w* is silent.

When a word has two vowels next to each other, the sound is that of the long first one.

We don't want to just throw a strategy at students. It's best to wait until the strategy comes up naturally in reading or writing. Then discuss it together. A "Word Attack Log" (see next page) makes a great Student Study Folder as described in Chapter 1. The students will each need a two-pocket folder with notebook paper. As strategies appear naturally in the course of reading and writing, they should be added, along with sample words.

## Word Attack Log

Strategy: _____

Sample words:

_____     _____     _____
_____     _____     _____
_____     _____     _____

Strategy: _____

Sample words:

_____     _____     _____
_____     _____     _____
_____     _____     _____

# Introductory Lesson

Say to students something like, "Is it possible for us to know how to spell every word in the English language?" (Wait—you'll get giggles and rolling eyes as the students say NO!)

"You know, I think maybe you're forgetting something! I agree that probably none of us could memorize how to spell every word. Why would we even want to? But is it possible for us to know how to spell them all with the help of one book? What is that book? Of course, the dictionary. What a friendly, helpful book. It tells us what we need to know—and in such an organized way!

"But you know what? There are still words that we need to memorize. There are words we write and read regularly and we don't want to have to carry a dictionary everywhere we go! There are also words that go with subjects we are studying. It is important to be able to read, and then write about, the topics in our classes without referring to a dictionary. So do we all agree that there are words we just simply need to <u>know</u> how to spell?

"Lots of words belong to the same 'families' or they have letter groupings that are alike or similar (refer to Letter Groupings as appropriate). We're going to keep a Word Attack Log this year. In it we'll put rules and guidelines and spelling patterns. We'll call all of these our *Word Attack Strategies*. When we talk about a strategy, we'll think of words that use the strategy. Here's how it might work. I'm going to think aloud through an entry in our log. Listen closely."

### ◎ Think-Aloud

"I get so mixed up when I have to write words that have either (write on board, hesitantly) *ie* or *ei* in them. See—when I wrote the word *either* I had to stop and think. I always pronounce it with a long *e* sound but my grandmother used to say it with a long *i* sound. If I spelled it her way it might be "iether." Boy, does *that* look funny. I've never seen a rule that fits this one. But for other words with *ei* or *ie* I was taught a rule that says: (put up an overhead transparency of Word Attack Log and write the strategy)

Strategy: *i* before *e*, except after *c*, or when sounded as *a* as in *neighbor* or *weigh*

"Umm, kind of sounds like a song. I actually like to say it! Now I need to think of some words with the *ei* or *ie* combination. Let's see... (write in log as you use them) How about *chief*? There's no long *a* sound so it should be *ie*. Well, if I know how to spell *chief*, I must know how to spell *handkerchief* and *mischief* and... What about the words that rhyme with *chief*? I hear the long *e* sound. Boy, I sure wish *either* fit the rule, but it's one of those exceptions. The word *fierce* fits the rule. Now, how about another word like *neighbor* and *weigh*? I'll write *sleigh*. What about a word where the *ei* follows *c*? How about *receive*! Hey, this is fun!"

In addition to conducting spelling strategy think-alouds, keeping a word attack log, and having kids do the independent practice pages that follow, look for ways to keep spelling instruction a *shared* exploration. Research shows that the more students converse about words and their understandings, the more their spelling improves. Gather resources that include activities and practice pages kids can collaborate on. Two are listed below.

# Spelling and Grammar Books to Try

*Spellingworks!* and *Grammarworks!*, both by Jim Halverson, have lots of teaching strategies, exercises, student practice sheets, and mazes that kids love. (Scholastic, 1998, 1996).

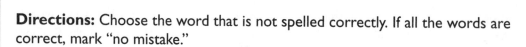

**Independent Practice for Grades 4 and 5**

# Spelling

Student
Page

**Directions:** Choose the word that is not spelled correctly. If all the words are correct, mark "no mistake."

1. A mess
   B seal
   C liquide
   D yoke
   E no mistake

2. J radar
   K bakteria
   L cliff
   M jacket
   N no mistake

3. A organizir
   B remind
   C hotel
   D indeed
   E no mistake

4. J foster
   K pain
   L leaven
   M maybe
   N no mistake

5. A accept
   B dispose
   C deth
   D elastic
   E no mistake

6. J tissue
   K increase
   L brother
   M weird
   N no mistake

7. A ninety
   B able
   C item
   D texture
   E no mistake

8. J biznis
   K absence
   L bother
   M neither
   N no mistake

9. A develop
   B tense
   C mispell
   D actor
   E no mistake

10. J minit
    K crease
    L blame
    M fortune
    N no mistake

11. A wisker
    B believe
    C arctic
    D garlic
    E no mistake

12. J blame
    K notion
    L maintain
    M elevate
    N no mistake

13. A actress
    B minimum
    C cupboard
    D vanilla
    E no mistake

14. J boyfriend
    K imatate
    L blame
    M burnt
    N no mistake

15. A author
    B telefone
    C memory
    D activity
    E no mistake

16. J gym
    K flower
    L panel
    M student
    N no mistake

Independent Practice for Grades 6, 7, 8

# Spelling

**Student Page**

**Directions:** Choose the word that is not spelled correctly. If all the words are correct, mark "no mistake."

**1.**
- A gasolene
- B actress
- C minor
- D lifestyle
- E no mistake

**2.**
- J authority
- K accepte
- L introduce
- M medical
- N no mistake

**3.**
- A candadate
- B minority
- C blameless
- D anticipate
- E no mistake

**4.**
- J candidate
- K torpedo
- L crumpeld
- M antique
- N no mistake

**5.**
- A ekwipped
- B actress
- C minor
- D everyone
- E no mistake

**6.**
- J increase
- K geography
- L perfectione
- M marriage
- N no mistake

**7.**
- A programmable
- B compleetly
- C momentary
- D probably
- E no mistake

**8.**
- J gigantic
- K memorial
- L benefactor
- M thereforle
- N no mistake

**9.**
- A citizenship
- B nazal
- C technical
- D impolite
- E no mistake

**10.**
- J wheelchair
- K average
- L utensil
- M success
- N no mistake

**11.**
- A nevertheless
- B mansion
- C bakteria
- D momentary
- E no mistake

**12.**
- J restarant
- K disappear
- L bureau
- M spectacular
- N no mistake

**13.**
- A eliminate
- B illustrate
- C decrease
- D prinsipal
- E no mistake

**14.**
- J distinguish
- K gitar
- L sensible
- M satisfactory
- N no mistake

**15.**
- A throughout
- B nonsense
- C nessesity
- D autograph
- E no mistake

**16.**
- J sandwich
- K jeopardy
- L junction
- M formidable
- N no mistake

Independent Practice for Grades 4 and 5

# Spelling

**Directions:** Circle the letter under the misspelled word in each sentence. If all the words are spelled correctly, circle the letter under "No mistake."

**1.** I <u>remember</u> that she was <u>frightened</u> by a <u>be</u>. <u>No mistake</u>
    A                B        C    D

**2.** To prepare <u>thoroughly</u> for the test, we should <u>review</u> our class notes and <u>homework</u>. <u>No mistake</u>.
            E                            F                      G        H

**3.** Sarah <u>happaly</u> <u>assisted</u> with the <u>housework</u> so her mother could take her shopping. <u>No mistake</u>
        A      B          C                                D

**4.** Robert Frost <u>advises</u> us to take the <u>rowed</u> less <u>traveled</u>. <u>No mistake</u>
                 E                  F        G         H

**5.** The <u>brightnes</u> of the sun was <u>less</u> <u>whenever</u> a cloud passed overhead. <u>No mistake</u>
         A                 B   C                      D

**6.** It would be a <u>mistack</u> to ride a <u>bicycle</u> without a <u>helmet</u>. <u>No mistake</u>
              E            F           G     H

**7.** Patrick <u>parked</u> his <u>automobile</u> near the <u>beach</u>. <u>No mistake</u>
        A        B           C      D

**8.** He <u>visited</u> his mother while the wind <u>quietly</u> rose to a <u>howl</u>. <u>No mistake</u>
        E                        F          G    H

**9.** The rain came, the wind <u>rose</u>, and the storm was <u>becomming</u> a <u>hurricane</u>. <u>No mistake</u>
                     A                      B     C     D

**10.** As the cloud <u>past</u> <u>overhead</u>, the rain fell in <u>huge</u> drops. <u>No mistake</u>
           E    F                    G        H

**Directions:** Choose the line that has a misspelled word. If all the words are spelled correctly, choose "No mistake."

**11.** A  As the storm passed,
      B  the rising water
      C  washed away his car.
      D  No mistake

**12.** E  Should we of think Patrick as carless
      F  rather then
      G  careless?
      H  No mistake

**13.** A  Hurricanes and
      B  cyclones are
      C  diferent types of the same storm.
      D  No mistake

**14.** E  There were
      F  violent storms with high
      G  winds and lots of rain.
      H  No mistake

**15.** A  On a map, villages,
      B  towns, and
      C  citys all have different symbols.
      D  No mistake

**16.** E  As the population
      F  gets larger,
      G  more of the circle is filled in.
      H  No mistake

**17.** A  If a large industry
      B  brings many jobs, a village may
      C  becum a town almost overnight.
      D  No mistake

**18.** E  The course
      F  fabric caused Samantha
      G  to itch and scratch all day.
      H  No mistake

Name _____ Date _____

**Independent Practice for Grades 4 and 5**

# Spelling

Student
Page

**Directions:** Circle the letter under the misspelled word in each sentence. If all the words are spelled correctly, circle the letter under "No mistake."

1. The school nurse <u>refered</u> all <u>injured</u> students to the town's <u>newest</u> doctor. <u>No mistake</u>
   A          B                C       D

2. The old one-room school had a <u>bathroom</u> in a <u>separate</u> building with no <u>running</u> water. <u>No mistake</u>
   E        F            G         H

3. The teacher <u>enforced</u> strict <u>obediens</u> with a great <u>twig</u> she called a switch. <u>No mistake</u>
   A        B         C       D

4. President Andrew Jackson's <u>portrait</u> is off <u>center</u> on the new 20-<u>dolar</u> bill. <u>No mistake</u>
   E        F           G        H

5. The new 20-dollar bills have several other <u>features</u> that make them <u>difficult</u> to <u>counterfiet</u>. <u>No mistake</u>
   A         B       C       D

6. The blowing snow made keeping the <u>rowed</u> clear a <u>difficult</u> task for the snow <u>plows</u>. <u>No mistake</u>
   E        F         G       H

7. One third of the <u>sophmore</u> class was <u>absent</u> with the flu <u>virus</u>. <u>No mistake</u>
   A        B        C    D

8. <u>Imaginery</u> friends are normal for young <u>children</u> but <u>abnormal</u> for adults. <u>No mistake</u>
   E            F        G        H

9. Mark's <u>unlocked</u> car was stolen. Was he <u>carless</u> or <u>careless</u>? <u>No mistake</u>
   A          B      C     D

10. <u>Sincerly</u> is the most <u>commonly</u> used closing in a <u>business</u> letter. <u>No mistake</u>
    E        F         G       H

**Directions:** Choose the line that has a misspelled word. If all the words are spelled correctly, choose "No mistake."

11. A   Students and their parents
    B   painted the school libary
    C   over the weekend.
    D   No mistake

12. E   Julie's great aunt lost
    F   her savings in a bank failure
    G   during the Great Depression.
    H   No mistake

13. A   Rachel's father celebrated
    B   his birthday
    C   at home when he turned fourty.
    D   No mistake

14. E   Colds are caused by a virrus;
    F   infected cuts
    G   result from bacteria.
    H   No mistake

15. A   The aroma of bacon
    B   cooking on the campfire lead
    C   the bear to the campsite.
    D   No mistake

16. E   The pitcher threw the
    F   baseball so hard, it went through
    G   the webbing on the cather's mitt.
    H   No mistake

17. A   In many schools you cant
    B   play sports unless
    C   you maintain a C average.
    D   No mistake

18. E   Mr. Gomez was anxious to
    F   way the tuna his son caught on
    G   his first day of helping his dad.
    H   No mistake

# Test-Taking Tips for Spelling

**1** Read directions very carefully. Are you looking for the word that is spelled **correctly** or the one that is **misspelled**?

**2** Decide if the word **looks right**.

**3** If you know how a word sounds, look for examples of **spelling rules** like "i before e," "double consonants follow short vowel sounds," etc.

**4** **Look for familiar letter groupings.** Are prefixes, suffixes, rhyming groups used correctly?

**5** **Be aware of homophones.** A word may be spelled correctly, but not be the correct spelling for the context in which it is used. For instance, the underlined word in "She sat in a window seat on the <u>plain</u>" would not be misspelled if it were by itself in a list. It is misspelled in the context of the sentence. Read for sentence context!

**6** If you are asked to choose the word that is spelled correctly from a list of words, **eliminate the words you know are misspelled** and if more than one is left, choose the word that looks most familiar.

# Final Thoughts

I hope this book has shown you that a positive attitude, and some direct instruction on test-taking strategies, goes a long way toward promoting student success.

As humans (or superhumans, as some hold the standard for teachers), we naturally approach tasks in different ways depending on our attitudes. Creative and resourceful educators have the capability to turn the test-preparation process into a positive experience for students while achieving high test score results. On a daily basis, teachers face and overcome challenges and obstacles for the good of their students. Dealing with the dilemma of standardized testing should be no exception.

All the pieces are in place to turn what many dread and view as a disjointed puzzle, into a picture of success. States want schools to be successful, although they may needlessly restrict some legitimate forms of preparation. Districts certainly value high success percentages, although they, too, may unnecessarily inhibit effective preparation. Building administrators know that the reputations of their schools, as well as funding allocations, rest with test results. They often provide extra training and manpower to aid teachers in test preparation in whatever form it may take. Publishers offer lists of objectives and skills that will be tested, along with samples of the formats to be utilized. And best of all, teachers are armed with previous years' results to diagnose strengths and weaknesses. The pieces of the puzzle are just waiting to be assembled!

While policy makers grapple with the "do we or don't we" of standardized testing, and publishers attempt to make both the content and format of tests in the image of what is considered best practice, the classroom teacher has daily responsibility to make this requirement beneficial to students. Rather than allowing the current system to depress or overwhelm, teachers should take a proactive stance and turn standardized testing into a positive experience. With team planning, creativity, and encouragement, test preparation can be an ongoing and intertwined layer of instruction.

Bottom line: Make test preparation a natural, integral part of what we do in the classroom! Students will learn more content, become more flexible, and reap the benefits of success.

# Answers

Vocabulary: Synonyms and Antonyms
Teacher-Directed Student Practice (pages 24–25)

1. b
2. c
3. b
4. a
5. a
6. c
7. c
8. d

Vocabulary: Synonyms and Antonyms
Independent Practice: Phrases (page 26)

1. C
2. B
3. D
4. A
5. A
6. D
7. C
8. B

Vocabulary: Synonyms and Antonyms
Independent Practice: Sentences (page 27)

1. C
2. H
3. A
4. H
5. B
6. G
7. D
8. G

Vocabulary: Multiple Meaning Words
Teacher Directed Student Practice (pages 30–31)

1. D
2. F
3. D
4. E

Vocabulary: Multiple Meaning Words
Independent Practice 1 (page 32)

1. B
2. G
3. C
4. G
5. B
6. G
7. D
8. E

Vocabulary: Multiple Meaning Words
Independent Practice 2 ( page 33)

1. B
2. E
3. D
4. G
5. D
6. G
7. B
8. G

Vocabulary: Words in Phrases: Pair Practice Activity
(page 36)

1. B
2. A
3. D
4. A
5. D
6. A

Vocabulary: Words in Paragraphs
Independent Practice (page 37)

1. D
2. B
3. A
4. C
5. B
6. D

Reading Comprehension: Grades, 4, 5
Independent Practice I (pages 46–47)

1. B
2. Korea, yes
3. B
4. the communists had taken over their part of the country
5. Seoul, South
6. D
7. B

Reading Comprehension: Grades 4, 5
Independent Practice 2 (page 48)

1. boat
2. Island, peninsula
3. Miguel and Tomas
4. About 50 feet
5. To maintain their reputation
6. Torres
7. Because the Torres brothers fished there

Reading Comprehension: Grades, 6, 7, 8
Independent Practice I (pages 52–53)

1. to ask their opinions
2. No, he says he doesnít
3. No, he thanks him for all he has done
4. C
5. Yes, because of the nature way the letter is written
6. B

Reading Comprehension: Grades, 6, 7, 8
Independent Practice 2 (page 54)

1. D
2. B
3. Something thought to be true but is not
4. Study Impressionist painting

Reading Comprehension: Grades, 6, 7, 8
Independent Practice 3 (page 56)

1. D
2. It was cold
3. C
4. D
5. A
6. Newspapers, the shoes are too big

Capitalization: Grades 4-8
Identifying Mistakes
Independent Practice I page 62)

1. D
2. J
3. C
4. I
5. B
6. G
7. C
8. J

Capitalization: Grades 4-8
Identifying Mistakes
Independent Practice 2 (page 63)

1. A
2. F
3. B
4. G
5. D
6. G
7. C
8. E

Capitalization: Grades 4-8
Filling in the Blank
Independent Practice (pages 64–65)

1. E
2. B
3. E
4. B
5. H
6. C
7. H
8. A

Punctuation: Grades 4-8
Missing Punctuation
Independent Practice (page 71)

1. D
2. G
3. C
4. H
5. A
6. H
7. B
8. G
9. B
10. J

Punctuation: Grades 4-8
Replacing Phrases
Independent Practice (pages 72–73)

1. D
2. K
3. B
4. G
5. E
6. F
7. C
8. G

Punctuation: Grades 4-8
Identifying Mistakes
Independent Practice (pages 74–75)

1. C
2. F
3. A
4. F
5. D
6. F
7. C
8. G
9. C
10. H
11. B
12. E

Punctuation: Grades 4-8
Filling in the Blanks
Independent Practice (pages 76-77)

1. B
2. H
3. A
4. E
5. C
6. F
7. A
8. E
9. D
10. G

Language Arts Mechanics
Overview with Sample ( pages 78–79)

1. B
2. E
3. C
4. E
5. B
6. G

Language Arts Mechanics: Grades 4-8
TerraNova/MAT
Independent Practice 1 (pages 80–81)

1. D
2. G
3. A
4. E
5. B
6. E
7. B
8. G
9. D

Language Arts Mechanics: Grades 4-8
TerraNova/MAT
Independent Practice 2 (pages 82–83)

1. C
2. D
3. C
4. B
5. C
6. D
7. C
8. C
9. D

Language Arts Expression: Grades 4-8
Filling in the Blank
Independent Practice (pages 90–91)

1. B
2. F
3. C
4. F
5. B
6. H
7. A
8. E

Language Arts Expression: Grades 4-8
Identifying Mistakes
Independent Practice (pages 92–93)

1. F
2. C
3. E
4. B
5. E
6. A
7. E
8. B
9. E
10. A

Language Arts Expression: Grades 4-8
Word and Phrase Replacement
Independent Practice (pages 94–95)

1. F
2. A
3. F
4. C
5. E
6. A
7. H
8. A
9. E

Language Arts Expression: Grades 4-8
Subject and Predicate
Independent Practice (page 96)

1. E
2. B
3. G
4. C
5. B
6. G
7. D
8. G

Language Arts Expression: Grades 4-8
Combining Sentences
Independent Practice (pages 100–101)

1. D
2. D
3. D
4. A
5. B
6. C
7. A
8. D
9. B

Language Arts Expression: Grades 4-8
Choosing Topic Sentences
Independent Practice (page 105)

1. C
2. A
3. A
4. B

Spelling
Independent Practice: Grades 4–5 (page 118)

1. C
2. K
3. A
4. N
5. C
6. N
7. E
8. J
9. C
10. J
11. A
12. N
13. E
14. K
15. B
16. N

Spelling
Independent Practice: Grades 6, 7, 8 (page 119)

1. A
2. K
3. A
4. L
5. A
6. L
7. B
8. M
9. B
10. N
11. C
12. J
13. D
14. K
15. C
16. N

Spelling
Independent Practice: Grades 4–5 (page 120)
1. C
2. H
3. A
4. F
5. A
6. E
7. D
8. H
9. B
10. E
11. D
12. F
13. C
14. H
15. C
16. H
17. C
18. E

Spelling
Independent Practice: Grades 4–5 (page 121)
1. A
2. H
3. B
4. G
5. D
6. E
7. A
8. E
9. D
10. E
11. B
12. H
13. C
14. E
15. B
16. G
17. A
18. F